# PC MANAGEMENT

## A How-To-Do-It Manual for Selecting, Organizing, and Managing Personal Computers in Libraries

## MICHAEL SCHUYLER
## JAKE HOFFMAN

*HOW-TO-DO-IT MANUALS*
*FOR LIBRARIES*
*Number 6*

*Series Editor: Bill Katz*

NEAL-SCHUMAN PUBLISHERS, INC.
New York, London  1990

Published by Neal-Schuman Publishers, Inc.
23 Leonard Street
New York, NY 10013

Copyright © 1990 by Michael Schuyler

Printed and bound in the United States of America

**Library of Congress Cataloging-in-Publication Data**

Schuyler, Michael
    PC management : a how-to-do-it manual for librarians / Michael
Schuyler, Jake Hoffman.
        p.       cm. — (How to do it manuals for librarians ; no. 6)
    ISBN 1-55570-076-4
    1. Microcomputers—Library applications—Handbooks, manuals, etc.
2. Libraries—Automation--Handbooks, manuals, etc.   I. Title.
II. Series.
Z678.93.M53S38   1990
025'00285       536—dc20                              90-5522
                                                        CIP

To my mother-in-law, Pauline Gardner, who
loves computers. May she always be online.

# CONTENTS

# SERIES EDITOR'S PREFACE

Personal computers are proliferating in libraries and other professional and business institutions. Even a small library can wind up with a dozen or so PCs—often different brands, using different software and not necessarily on speaking terms with each other. By automating many functions, PCs help the besieged professional to spend more time actually running the library or department and less time poring over various aspects of record keeping and such.

Michael Schuyler, PC guru and librarian extraordinaire, is the perfect guide through this electronic labyrinth. He follows the success of *Now What? How to Get Your Computer Up and Keep It Running* (Neal-Schuman, 1988) with another significant contribution to the understanding and use of computers. In exceptionally readable, easy-to-follow, yet precise and logical language, *PC Management* takes the reader through a general overview of PCs, and then goes on to explain everything you ever wanted to know about making the interface between and among PCs uniform. Schuyler continues on to applications, managing various PC configurations, and then discusses hardware, software, CD-ROM, and the tools and supplies needed to keep it all going. As a bonus, he offers readers a free disk containing a PC management program to get them started.

It's all done with a smile, backed up by serious experience and mastery of the art of the computer. The result is a must-have guide for anyone who is trying to forge a smoothly functioning PC system out of a multitude of disparate units.

*Bill Katz*

# PREFACE

People used to think I was a PC Guru (They know better now). And the only reason for that was that I had an Apple at home that I programmed to do astrology charts. It was a great way to get to know people. Then I sold my motorcycle to get enough money to buy a disk drive. I guess I was hooked.

So I wound up six months ahead of everyone else in knowing what computers could do. Naturally, when people in my organization decided they might like to purchase a microcomputer, they asked me what I thought.

I thought they should get an Apple just like mine. Besides, there weren't many other choices out there. IBM was still deciding whether or not they were interested, and, well, I didn't know how to use any other computers.

Within a year or two all sorts of office functions had become automated. There was a payroll program that did all sorts of salary manipulations; and quite a few spreadsheets that eased the drudgery of record keeping. Since the machine had a special "CP/M" card installed, we could learn dBase II and Wordstar and a few programs not designed for the Apple as well.

When we decided to purchase a second microcomputer, things were still OK. After all, it was easy to memorize what was in them, both hardware and software. There wasn't that much there; and I was the only one who knew how to use the original Apple.

But things got out of hand. Critical mass for me was about a dozen micros. At that I point I began to forget what cards were in which slots and what version of which software was on what hard disk. I was having head crashes all the time. The new circulation system had also grown to 100 terminals; and that didn't help matters, either. Also, there was a mixture of Apples and IBMs, which weren't exactly compatible; and that's putting it nicely.

*PC Management: A How-To-Do-It Manual For Librarians* was written partly out of desperation, really, and partly out of a desire to warn others they should watch out before microcomputers took over their offices and back rooms everywhere.

At a dozen computers I needed help in organizing just what was going on in the organization. It doesn't matter if you can handle half that amount or double without a system. Eventually you, too, will reach critical mass and need to organize, to manage the entire micro process.

This book attempts to offer real, specific recommendations on what programs to use system wide. In some sense we're sticking our neck out recommending one piece of software over another. There are always people who use the alternative who will attack such an approach because their favorite was not chosen.

But the usual banal recommendation of "use whatever meets your needs best" has always struck us as the easy way out for the person giving the answer, but the most frustrating to hear by the person asking the question.

Think of it. You ask what data base system is best; and your expert answers,

"Oh, dBase or R:Base or Paradox or Revelation, or maybe First Choice. They're really all quite adequate. Or maybe Hypercard, depending."

Do you want to hear that?

Not me. I want someone to quit weaseling and take a stand. The fact is there is no wrong answer, so it won't hurt to take a side.

In fact, we're most likely to choose a software program not based on our personal favorite, but on the idea that there is some comfort in choosing a package that is known and used by a wide variety of people all over the country. The fact is, if you get in trouble, it will be much easier to find someone who can understand and program in dBase than in a homebrew specialized application written in RPG, such as our newspaper indexing program. This was written by a person who has since decided to further his education in graduate school. His company no longer exists, and we are faced with supporting compiled code (no source code) for a program that still has numerous bugs.

Other factors include budget, believe it or not, and the ability to perform the job.

The point, really, is that we suspect you want answers to questions regarding setting up not just a PC, but a PC program. Having done it more than once, this is how we would do it next time.

Chapter One presents the framework for PC Management. It discusses the issue of PC support for an organization adding micros all the time; and the problems and choices available for interfaces and uniformity.

Chapter Two presents the Uniform Interface, a way to make computers consistent within the organization. If an employee can use one computer, he or she can use them all, even if they have different programs running on them.

Chapter Three presents an applications toolbox of software which we recommend for use with MS-DOS computers. We take a stand. We tell you why. These programs work. If you have other favorites, fine. At least we are taking a stand. We aren't telling you to get "whatever."

The Applications Toolbox includes not just user programs like word processors. It also includes diagnostic utilities and programs to help you as the Guru-designate in solving problems, writing those nifty little batch routines, and helping to prevent disaster. Recommendations for these toolbox programs are given as well; and utilities are compared and contrasted.

Chapter Four covers Configuration Management and includes a description of a complete and ready-to-run PC Management program called "PC TENDER" available to purchasers of this book free of charge. Send us a disk (and a stamp or two) and we send you the program ready to implement at your site.

We've seen programs like this sold for $2,000. Maybe ours isn't as fancy, but it works for us and it will work for you in attempting to keep track of all those computers and software packages.

Chapter Five covers the issue of Software Policy in an organization under growth pressure for new PCs. A sample software policy is provided. It can protect the organization and employees against software theft and unauthorized use. It ought to be passed by every Board of Trustees in the country. It shows you're paying attention.

Chapter Six covers the issue of support. How many PCs will it take before you can get more help? How many is it reasonable for one person to maintain. Guidelines are given. Figures from industry are provided; and a formula for computing your own needs for support is offered.

Chapter Seven covers hardware possibilities. Which type of computer should you buy? What computer choices will lock you out of any future upgrades as the industry marches on? And which ones are reasonable to purchase when your needs are modest? We'll tell you what we think, including specific brand names.

Chapter Eight is a contribution by Jake Hoffman, Microcomputer Consultant for the state of Idaho, on CD-ROM, a subject that can enthrall and frustrate us all within seconds of each other. The specific recommendations and techniques here can make it much easier for you to deal with CD-ROM, particularly when you have more than one disk from more than one publisher to use on only one PC.

Chapter Nine discusses tools and supplies, two broad areas requiring adequate attention. A basic hardware toolbox is listed, and vendors of after-market supplies are contrasted and compared. Addresses for sources of parts are given.

Chapter Ten details the free disk offer for the PC Tender, the configuration management program designed to help you keep track of PCs. If you're willing to supply postage and a mailer, we'll just send you the disk of the working program, source code included, free. We'd also like you to fill out a short questionnaire for us, but that's optional.

# 1 PC MANAGEMENT: AN INTRODUCTION

To any organization of any size, micros must be like guppies. At first they must have seemed small and inconsequential compared to the mainframe "big fish" of the corporate environment, but suddenly there were guppies everywhere. If they weren't authorized, then employees bought them and brought them on their own. Suddenly, everything from memos to full-fledged reports had that dot-matrix look of computer assistance.

Surely this has recently been no great surprise. After all, *Time* magazine made a computer "Man of the Year" quite awhile ago. The fact that micros have arrived is not so much at issue as what to do with them as they proliferate beyond the boundaries of control and support.

Control and support are opposite sides to the same coin, as socialist countries such as the U.S.S.R. are quick to point out. To the question of a lack of personal freedom in many of these states, the reply is that everyone has a job.

Not to put too fine a point on it, but corporate structures have often resembled this socialist paradigm internally while enjoying the benefits of capitalism externally. *Glasnost* is not a fundamental concept within the corporate world. Indeed, computers themselves have often been enlisted to serve the corporate need for control by measuring output, logging phone calls (to whom, how long, how much) and Byzantine password control structures (enter your barcode now).

Micros, of course, point out this small paradox quite adroitly. Here you have individual employees increasing their own productivity by circumventing what can often be a glacial corporate computer structure. No technology has so well embodied the sixties slogan "Power to the People" as the micro. Yes, the "disadvantaged classes" still cannot afford the grand or more it takes to partake of the entry level of serious computing. But the fact is that micros have brought more computer power lower down the economic spectrum and into the hands of more people than any revolution since that of electricity. Computers have become appliances.

After a short period of resistance, most corporate cultures have adopted micros as an essential office productivity tool. There may still be enclaves where it is considered bad form to read *Byte* magazine, but by and large the micro revolution is over. They won.

And corporate interest in control of the micro is not always as Machiavellian as it sounds. As one corporate data processing executive put it, "Sure, you have all these employees demanding to buy any damn piece of software they choose. As a result, we have fifteen different word processors scattered throughout ten states. And when someone has a problem, who do they call? Me!"

Such sentiment is as much a reason for "approved software lists" as any attempt to pull in the reins of control. The issue is support.

## SUPPORT

For the moment, let us ignore the "control" aspect of the corporate vision of micros and concentrate on the support issue. As an appliance, micros must be supported in a way that benefits the user and increases his or her productivity. With this central idea in mind, one can structure a support program that accomplishes this major goal while succeeding in providing justification and true benefit to the corporation as well. This is not an idle or cursory point. The health of the corporation is important. The entire philosophy here is that increasing individual productivity will in turn increase corporate productivity. It is a symbiotic relationship.

Support would not be as much of a problem with microcomputers if we were always dealing with a literate population of users. The population is literate in many things, of course, from how to drive automobiles to how to use a telephone. Not much effort need be placed in training users for these operations. It has been done by others.

Computer literacy has become a cliché of sorts as the culture has attempted to deal with the issues involved. One school of thought feels that machinery needs to be made user-friendly so that users won't have problems controlling it. Just like automobiles. If you can drive a manual transmission (a feat requiring an initiation phase, hopefully in a large parking lot) you can drive just about anything on wheels, even trucks. The "user interface" is the same. Of course a bus is different from a Volkswagen, but the problems associated with this transition are mostly psychological, as the driver learns to extend consciousness and awareness further to the side and behind. In any case, a driver, in theory, is using an automobile as an appliance to arrive at a certain location. The object of the exercise is not to drive the car, but to get somewhere.

The opposite view is embodied by the maxim, "Build a system a fool could use, and only a fool will use it." The idea is that in order to make things absurdly easy for the users, you must strait-jacket them into a way of using computers that limits their use. Both ideas have points to be made.

## THE INTERFACE PROBLEM

This "user-friendly" school would have the computer's user interface be as simple as possible. The simpler the interface, the greater number of people will be able to use computers. Certainly the largest single complaint of new computer users is that they are too hard to learn to use. The user is faced with mastering a complete set of rules, a completely new environment *before* being allowed to run the actual programs with which to increase productivity. This environment is seen as cryptic and diversionary, deflecting the user from the true purpose of using the computer in the first place.

Stories abound of children learning to use the Macintosh computer, for example, which has a graphic and icon-based interface which, when coupled with a mouse, allows non-verbal use of computers. It is the kind of interface, and Apple is the kind of computer, that users tend to fall in love with. It engenders fierce loyalty; some treat the computer, and the company, as a religion, not an appliance.

Apple Computer has taken advantage of these attitudes in the past. In one famous commercial, a young woman dressed in red and white with the Apple logo on her T-shirt, smashes a hammer through the grimacing face of Big Brother, only to awaken the downtrodden masses to their oppression. In another commercial, Apple has a line of besuited executives cum briefcases walking off a cliff, lemming-like, in conformity with IBM. Apple, the computer for the rest of us. Lately, Apple has spurned this approach in favor of courting corporate executives with the "man buys Macintosh, keeps job" approach, along with some significant help from Aldus' Pagemaker and desktop publishing for the Macintosh. Nevertheless, there remains a brisk market in lapel pins with a circle and "X" through MS-DOS. "Just say No!" they proclaim.

Not to be outdone, Microsoft has presented Windows, a new operating environment that runs on top of MS-DOS ("messy-DOS") and transforms the typical MS-DOS computer into a very Macintosh-looking desktop environment. The resemblance is so close, in fact, that Apple and Microsoft, along with Hewlett Packard, are involved in a massive lawsuit over the very issue of copyrighted user interfaces. Meanwhile Xerox, the company from which Apple originally "borrowed" the entire idea, has decided to jump into the fray by suing Apple for the original appropriation. But while Apple claims Microsoft is guilty of stealing the interface from them, they maintain their innocence in stealing it from Xerox. OS/2, the newest operating system from Microsoft and IBM, will have a Presentation Manager, which is an off-shoot of Windows and is probably the real target of Apple's suit. It is clear that if

Microsoft and IBM have anything to say about it, the Windows-type of interface will be around for a long time.

Indeed, there appears to be rush toward the user-friendly desktop metaphor, called "GUI" for "Graphics User Interface," as well as applications themselves which are even more friendly than the desktop. Intrinsic in this idea is that graphics-based systems allow a greater population of users and that a greater population of users is good and beneficial. But this approach just may beg the question entirely, as the following story illustrates.

I have this on good authority that the story is not apocryphal. (Thank you, Jim Kolb.) Some friends were staying in Hawaii, in Honolulu, when the power went out in the part of the city where they were. This was at dinner time, and no one could use a stove. Discovering that a McDonald's restaurant in another part of the city was open, they seized upon this opportunity for a meal.

When they arrived at the restaurant, they found long lines at the counter. Although power was working in this part of the city, it seems the computer for the McDonald's cash registers was in the part of the city they had just left. Therefore, the cash registers were not working.

Now, if you've ever peeked over the registers at one of these places, you see not numbers, but pictures. If you order a Big Mac, the attendant presses a picture of a Big Mac. If you order French fries, a picture of French fries is depressed. Because the menu is rather limited, there is a picture for every product. If you order two Big Macs, they just press the picture twice. This all adds up internally, of course, and gives you an automatic total owed. You give the attendant a $10 bill, and change is automatically computed as well. It's all automatic.

Except this time the registers didn't work. The crew at McDonald's had managed to get the registers open and were attempting to serve food to the many people who all had the same idea of having a meal when the power was out.

The problem was that the attendants could not add and subtract; and they could not make change. Not only were the attendants in this predicament, but their first-line supervisors also could not add; they could not subtract; they could not make change.

To save this situation from becoming a disaster of major proportions, someone had enlisted the aid of several customers (older women, we're told) who had attended school when knowing how to add, subtract, and make change were prerequisites for graduation. It was these older people who were helping the attendants cope and allowing the people to be fed.

No one can say that these cash registers were not user-friendly.

Even people who were otherwise illiterate could be placed in a position where they were using computers in a productive and efficient manner. They were trained by VCRs in all the techniques necessary to master the craft.

It is an extreme approach, welcomed by at least some corporations. Most of the time, it works. Some will even claim that the people using the cash registers with pictures on them are "using computers." In the literal sense, they are; but the question then becomes: Are they understanding their use of computers?

No, they're not. They have been insulated entirely from the computer to the point that they know no more information than it takes to process the words "Big Mac" from a customer's mouth into the depression of a Big Mac picture on the keyboard. Presumably, even this phase could be automated. Voice recognition systems are being steadily improved. And this system certainly works the other way around. Our local grocery store has a talking cash register that voices the product and the price after the clerk rubs the bar code over the laser scanner. If these systems were perfected, the ultimate computer interface would be speech, and the human intermediary could be abandoned. Or, at least, it would move one step further out, to the consumer interfacing with the microphone.

From a social perspective, this touch of human engineering has another problem. The people pushing the Big Mac buttons may not have been able to slog though the educational system, or perhaps the educational system did not teach them how to think without the crutch of a calculator. There are countless other possibilities. Let us not assign blame at this point. Others revel in this sort of analysis anyway.

But this does not mean that these "computer users" don't have a brain. Circumventing the problems of education by accepting them, then designing around these problems with technology may be enhancing the quality of life for corporations, but surely not for the individuals singled out for use in this manner, at the minimum wage.

A technical solution is easier for companies in this position because intrinsic social questions need not be answered. In some sense, then, the corporate use of the Big Mac interface is elitist. It begs the question of educating employees by designing around their lack of education. Besides, if they were educated, we'd have to pay them more.

There is another school of thought. One of its proponents is George Morrow, once chairman of Morrow Designs, a now-defunct computer maker, that was known for high-quality CP/M machines. For many reasons, his company did not survive the transition to 16 bits and MS-DOS. And certainly, none of his machines ever ran Windows.

Dr. Morrow is not a fan of graphics-based interfaces. He maintains that interfaces tending in this direction have several built-in limitations. For McDonald's, it means their menu selection will be forever limited by the number of pictures on their cash registers. Therefore, the technology is driving the breadth of their product offerings. Pictures, such as the Egyptians used in hieroglyphics, simply do not offer the breadth of combinations necessary to express the breadth of ideas necessary. That's why hieroglyphics died out in favor of a writing system that used arbitrary symbols, in combination called an "alphabet," which has many advantages over the icon system of representing ideas. You can imagine Dr. Morrow's opinion of user-interfaces such as Windows in combination with pointing devices such as the mouse. He doesn't like them, declaring them a step backwards.

The extreme edge of this view would be a command-line interface, in English, which directed the computer what to do. Just like MS-DOS, CP/M before it, and Apple's nearly-but-not-quite departed DOS 3.3, the DOS for the Apple II series before ProDos. The command line interface gives the user quite a lot of power. For programmers, it's great. No Windows are in the way. You're looking at the innards, the raw guts of the computer.

Well, not quite. Actually, any Disk Operating System is a "window" of a sort and hardly at the lowest level of computer interfacing. Someone had to program the operating system to present a letter on the CRT when you typed it on the keyboard. That's neither automatic nor intrinsic; it was programmed.

The entire operation is on a continuum anyway. The lowest level is the zero/one combination in the microcode imbedded in the integrated chips that do all the work. Few people can muck around at this level. The next level up is machine language itself, still with zeros and ones, but this time mostly converted to hexadecimal, for ease of use, if you can believe that. The number 20, for example, might, in a crucial location, mean to jump to a subroutine. Then there's assembly language, a collection of mnemonic codes that manipulate the zeroes and ones. Assembly is easier than strictly machine language, but it really is a window into machine language rather than a program that isolates you from machine language. "JMP" replaces 20, but the 20 appears on the screen right beside it anyway.

Now we come to the operating system itself, written in some sort of language and compiled, that insulates the user from the zeroes and ones. Oriented particularly to manipulating files on disk drives, the operating system, to some programmers, is as much of a burden as Windows is to others. You can't easily program machine language from the operating systems. The tools simply are not there to help you. It's like trying to accomplish woodworking with tools found in a metal shop; there are some similarities, but the fit makes life difficult.

Past the operating system we come upon development languages such as "C", BASIC, and Fortran. These reside on top of the operating system, or in conjunction with it. They have little trap-doors so you can peer into machine language occasionally, but their user interface is several steps higher than manipulating at the bit level. Programmers, in the traditional sense, write programs in these languages for the end user to use. Some results of writing in these languages lead to still other languages such as dBase, itself a perfectly robust and helpful applications language.

In fact, many products may have origins in many languages. Once compiled into machine language, the origin disappears, except for telltale signs recognized only by programmers. Thus dBase was originally a machine language product and is now written in "C".

Windows, and the Macintosh Finder, Desqview, GEM, and other operating systems place a veneer over the operating system, thus further insulating us from the guts of the computer. But the major point is that we are all insulated at some level from the computer itself. The interfaces available to the user of computers in a corporate environment, no matter what is used, is already several steps removed from the guts of the computer.

Nevertheless, Dr. Morrow comes down squarely on the side of the command-line interface. One learns this sort of interface by studying it, by trial and error, by becoming familiar with it.

Dr. Morrow, too, has had his share of criticism. Perhaps in line with his advocacy of the command-line interface, he also believes information about computers should not be promulgated by columnists whom he feels are mere users of computers. In one well-publicized foray, Morrow took on noted columnist Jerry Pournelle, probably the most famous computer columnist around. And Morrow got soundly walloped back, too, and was accused of being an elitist, among other things. But Pournelle is a professional writer; Morrow isn't. It wasn't a pretty sight.

The connection is that a command-line interface is also "elitist" in nature. Why? Because it requires a considerable amount of expert knowledge in order to be used properly. The command-line interface is the handle to rail against on Apple's "Computer for the

Rest of Us" campaigns. It's arcane, esoteric, and unnecessary. Why do you have to type "DELETE FILE" when you could just as well move a picture of that file to the picture of a garbage can on the screen with a mouse, and drop it in?

## THE SPECTRUM OF CHOICE

So at one end of the spectrum, we have the hieroglyphic Big Macs at McDonald's, which we have labeled elitist, and at the other, at least a character-oriented operating system, even though in reality it is nowhere near the bottom of the heap. And this, too, has been called elitist. One is too easy; the other is too hard, at least for the rest of us. For all intents and purposes, the argument is probably specious. Just because automatic transmissions were developed for automobiles to make them easier to drive does not mean that standard transmissions died out, even though that was an early prediction. They both exist, still, side-by-side, and gross judgments of culture and character do not depend upon their continued development. There is room for both, and both have their advantages, depending on the circumstances.

Nevertheless, it is from within this spectrum that we must choose to educate and support our own users of micros. It is perfectly possible to educate users at the MS-DOS level, for example. Microsoft sells cheaply an excellent DOS tutorial that, when paid attention to, can teach the user a great deal about the operating system, quite enough to impart a sense of competence at this level.

It is also perfectly possible to have users learn one applications program, and one only. This can be automatically started by the computer via an AUTOEXEC batch file, the HELLO program, or its equivalent. When the user turns the computer on, up pops the application program: a word processor, an accounting program, whatever serves the need. In theory, the program can be made to perform its own backups and other housekeeping. You can place it on automatic pilot. This is the same approach as is used on Mainframe and mini computers. A terminal runs a "job" or program. The accountants use the accounting program and have no idea how the job is run up or down, how the backup programs work, or how the reports are actually produced. It just sort of works, hopefully. How it works is up to the computer operators and programmers, who live and work in another room, or another building entirely. The terminal from which the program is used is dumb; it has no smarts of its own. In the newest vernacular, it is a "diskless workstation."

We shall assume that the vast population of potential computer users, particularly within the corporate environment, falls somewhere between the Big Mac interface and the command-line interface. The difference between PCs and the workstation concept is that with PCs, the entire computer is in a box on the desk. That opens up many new possibilities.

For new users, the choice may be as much how you spend the resources as anything. Educating users about the DOS prompt and allowing them to move files around and manipulate their micros at the DOS level will be more costly up-front, but will result in a population of more educated users. The automatic pilot approach will tend to limit the use of computers by users to the one application they are allowed. It does get them up and running on the application more quickly, but at a cost of understanding what they are doing. This isn't in the same league as the Big Mac interface, but on the spectrum of interfaces, it certainly is tending toward that direction.

This Interface spectrum is not quite as neat as Figure 1-1 implies. Like all simplifications, this leaves out some essential detail. For example, it is perfectly possible that the interface chosen is easier than the program itself. Windows running dBase is a

**FIGURE 1-1**

As the level of insulation from the real computer grows, the computer becomes more "user-friendly"

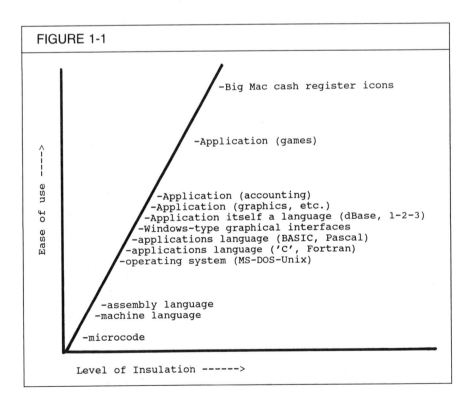

FIGURE 1-1

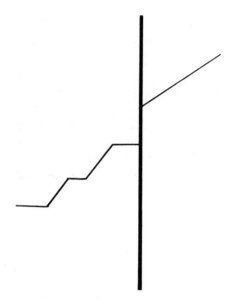

**FIGURE 1-2**

Adam Greene's "Wall" diagram depicting the difficulty of advancing in using dBase without learning to program in the dBase language. Only so much is possible using the interactive mode of the program.

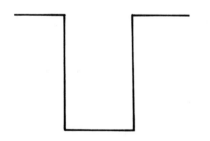

**FIGURE 1-3**

Adam Greene's "hole" diagram depicting what happens when a typical user installs a hard disk. It's a whole new world of sub-directories when this happens.

perfect example. dBase is a data base management system, or it is an applications language. You choose which one. As a data base management system, it leads you through creating and querying a data base, or it leaves you to flounder at the dot prompt (not to be confused with the DOS prompts, though they are cousins). Yet Windows is one of those warm, fuzzy interfaces that graphically gets you to open and close files on the desktop metaphor. It's like having a perfectly organized office with rows of neat file cabinets, color-coded and cross-referenced for easy retrieval. But once you open the file cabinet, the contents are in disarray, and the cat has claimed the corner to have her kittens. The neatness was an illusion.

Adam Green has developed a series of diagrams to explain the user's "interface" with various programs. He calls this "the wall" because you can steadily improve with your use of dBase only so far as a data base management system. Once you hit the wall, nothing else is possible until you learn to write programs in the dBase language. If you can get past the wall, the learning curve continues up. In fact, the dBase language is as robust as many below it. You can write an accounting or payroll program in dBase as easily as a program needing to organize vast quantities of data. If you stay in front of the wall, you can also manage, but not with the sophistication of a user turned programmer as he or she scaled the wall and traveled beyond.

More to the point, Adam Green also developed a diagram used to explain MS-DOS, the ubiquitous, if not popular interface for PC-type computers. This one is called the hole.

The hole arrives about the time you install a hard disk. You thought you knew how to copy and rename files, move them around, format disks, and run programs. Then you install a hard disk and find an entirely new level to DOS that requires a while to climb out of. Now there are sub-directories and duplicate file names to deal with, backups which are intrinsically more difficult. Indeed, what was once manageable on a 360K floppy has now become a vast sea of disk space: 20 megabytes, 30 megabytes, even more. Suddenly, you'll need a new program just to keep track of all the files on the disk. And as you finally figure out that all your applications can fit on one disk at one time and go faster than they have ever gone before, you'll need another disk because you filled the old one up.

Now, if you want to support an organization where employees enjoy productivity increases by programming their own applications in dBase, it might be considered overkill to install Windows on every last PC in the place. Why? If you can handle dBase DO

WHILE statements, Windows is just in the way. Yet you don't want to limit potential users of dBase by forcing them unwittingly into a level of insulation that may not be appropriate.

Besides, Windows, and the programs like it, are a cost to the organization, not just in the intrinsic cost of the programs themselves, but also the extra cost in increased memory and speed required to run them appropriately. Yet why subject your users to the horrors of the DOS hole if you don't have to? It's bad enough teaching people how to use an applications program without having to back off and teach them the intricacies of batch files and sub-directories before they can get any useful work done.

## THE UNIFORM INTERFACE

In the pages that follow, we will suggest a compromise approach for an organization that provides some semblance of continuity of approach, while allowing individual users the flexibility of exploring new areas from within a familiar environment. It doesn't do Windows, and it doesn't fall into the depths of DOS, even though that is the substance from which it is made. This Uniform Interface has several advantages.

1. It exerts some control, it is true; but it is easily circumvented and, in fact, encourages this approach.
2. It is "easier" to use than Windows and other similar interfaces because it makes their use for the moment unnecessary.
3. It allows the user to enter and use any applications program directly.
4. Because of the programs involved, it reminds users that there are other programs to explore.
5. Its uniformity of approach makes support of its contents easier for the support staff.
6. Its uniform style allows a sense of familiarity for anyone in the organization using any computer in the organization.
7. It's cheap to implement.
8. It's upward compatible. If you upgrade to a more powerful machine, the interface can follow right along.

We don't insist on a Uniform Interface for everyone. If you want to learn Spanish, don't pick up a book on French. But this is an approach that is working for us. It is just one of several choices available, including GUIs like Windows and the Macintosh, or even Character based systems as found in Wonder Plus, Hyperpad, or Desqview.

That's one of the neat things about micros. You get to choose.

# 2 UNIFORM INTERFACE

The Uniform Interface probably doesn't deserve capitals. It isn't sold anywhere, and no one agrees exactly on what it should look like. In fact, your uniform interface may be different from the uniform interface farther down the road. Like the Unified Field Theory, it is a concept we think is attainable, but no one has quite figured it out yet. There are quite a few theories that attempt it, even though none is perfect. Still, the search goes on.

By Uniform Interface, we mean an interface that is consistent within the organization. The basic concept is that the initial screens of all the computers in your organization will remain of the same type throughout. Any employee who walked up to any computer would be immediately familiar with how the computer worked and what was expected of him or her to run a program. Some of the applications programs might be the same as well, but that is not a requirement at this level (we'll talk about that later). The requirement is that you start a program the same way; and once you exit the program, the computer returns to a "known state" from which someone else can launch into an exploration of disk files, this time perhaps in a different direction.

There are several ways to accomplish a Uniform Interface. We present three of them here. The easiest can be done without any special "tools" at all. It's a Quick and Dirty approach, but it meets most of the requirements. The second way adds a few more refinements. The third method requires a small fifty dollar program called "Saywhat!?" that allows you to create a Uniform Interface that will be the envy of your friends and neighbors. Coupled with more complicated batches, the "Saywhat!?" interface might make people think you're a real programmer.

The computer industry has its own ideas of uniform interfaces. Windows, by Microsoft, is a good example. It copies from the Macintosh interface, which copies from the Xerox interface. All three of these use the so-called "desktop metaphor" to pretend the computer screen is the top of your desk, normally filled with file folders, notepads, and other tools. These are all "GUI" interfaces, which stands for "Graphics User Interfaces."

In the MS-DOS world, we believe GUI interfaces are not as well developed as they are in the Mac world. Although most any program can be made to work with something like Windows, there is usually a trade-off involved. First, it is simply not true that most programs are designed to work with Windows. Instead, Windows (and we're using this as an example) can accommodate other programs. As a result, a user invokes a program from Windows, but once running, the program behaves just like it would under a normal DOS environment.

The DOS version of Microsoft Word is the most ironic example. Though it can be invoked from Windows, it doesn't use Windows at all. Further, it will only run with Windows in what is called "text mode" rather than its more illustrative "graphics mode," which, of course, is one of the reasons for the existence of Windows in the first place. Further, Windows takes a great deal of RAM overhead. This limits the number of programs that can run with it within the normal 640K of the majority of installed machines.

Perhaps one day when all machines are 386 machines with megabytes of memory and a mouse attached, and when every publisher has a reasonable array of Windows-specific software to offer, then Windows will be a good choice as a Uniform Interface. We would not shun such a trend. But until that happens, we are suggesting Windows and its cousins can present yet another obstacle in the way of efficient computing within your organization.

In contrast, the Uniform interfaces take no special hardware, a small investment, if any, in software, and take up little memory space. This allows you to concentrate on the applications programs rather than the interface itself.

The interfaces below all assume you have a hard disk installed in the computer. If you don't have hard disks installed in your computers, do so. If you've never used a hard disk, you may not appreciate how life improves as a result of installing one. But the difference is exponential. Suddenly, all your programs can be online at once. You never have to worry about filling up a data disk. Other programs are instantly available. In addition, you will notice a dramatic speed increase in any operations involving disk access.

At one time, installing a hard disk represented a substantial investment. We remember installing a 10MB hard disk for $1100 for a friend; and we were happy to get 10MB instead of 5MB. Not any more. Hard disks for MS-DOS computers typically sell for $300 for 20 megabytes of space. We have seen the Seagate 225 hard disk sold for less than $250. The Seagate is a common work horse hard disk of medium speed. Certainly there are many more expensive, larger, and faster hard disks on the market, but compared to floppy drives, the Seagate is a screamer anyway. Another typical brand is Miniscribe.

# UNIFORM INTERFACE (VERSION ONE)

First, the simplified version. The Uniform Interface for MS-DOS type computers is based on batch files that are transparent to the user. There are three types of batch files to the scheme. The first type consists of an initial batch which invokes a menu. The second type is the menu itself. The third type actually does the work of running a program. Since you will probably have more than one program to run, there will be several clones of this third type of batch file, one for each program.

The initial file should probably be made into an AUTOEXEC.BAT file, unless you have a good reason for not doing so. Since alternatives require batches that call batches that call batches, it could all become very confusing in short order. The AUTOEXEC.BAT file executes automatically when you turn on the computer. If it displays a menu immediately, that is preferable. We shall assume such below:

THE AUTOEXEC.BAT file

```
prompt choice$g
echo off
cls
type menulist
```

The first line changes the DOS prompt to the word "CHOICE" plus the right-facing caret (That's what the $g means). The second line turns off ECHO, otherwise, each command would both execute and appear on the screen as a command, which we don't want. Thirdly, the batch clears the screen before it actually uses the DOS TYPE command to scroll MENULIST on the screen in line four.

Here the batch file simply displays choices on the screen. Because it has changed the DOS prompt, the usual "A>" prompt is replaced by a "choice>" prompt. The user types a single letter corresponding to the choices displayed. This letter invokes a second batch file which invokes the proper program. When the program terminates, the batch file is still in charge. It's last function is to recall the first batch file, which presents the choices on the screen once again.

This simplified interface has several advantages. The first is that it is so simple to implement. If you can write a simple batch file, then that's all you need. The TYPE command places the interface on the screen. The "CHOICE" prompt isn't anything more than a disguised DOS prompt, and all batches invoked by this procedure can be written with two or three lines. The first line runs the desired program. The second line runs the original batch again.

In this scenario the MENULIST file is a straight ASCII file that presents the choices available for a given computer. Here is a sample MENULIST file:

```
-----> Welcome to Idaho State Library <-----

        <W>   Microsoft Word
        <D>   dBase IV
        <P>   PC-Talk III
        <O>   OCLC terminal emulation
        <L>   Lotus 1-2-3
        <Q>   Quit to DOS

Please enter your choice from the list above
        and press [ENTER]
```

As you can see, the small batch file above changes the prompt, clears the screen, and types the file immediately above on the screen. The disguised DOS prompt appears below the typed document, so it all looks like it's from the same file. On the screen, these two programs working together look like this:

```
-----> Welcome to Idaho State Library <-----

        <W>   Microsoft Word
        <D>   dBase IV
        <P>   PC-Talk III
        <O>   OCLC terminal emulation
        <L>   Lotus 1-2-3
        <Q>   Quit to DOS

Please enter your choice from the list above
        and press [ENTER]

CHOICE>
```

Let's say the user typed in "W" to run Microsoft Word. The batch file to run WORD is also very simple. Let's assume Word is in a directory all it's own. The batch file is named "W.BAT" and it looks like this:

```
CD\WORD
WORD
CD\
AUTOEXEC
```

Once again, the file is very straightforward. Line One signs up to the WORD Directory. Line Two invokes the WORD program. Line Three signs back to the root directory after the user quits the Word program itself; and Line Four runs the original batch again so you're back where you started.

There are disadvantages to this approach. The major one is that you're not insulating your user from anything, really—you're just disguising it. The "CHOICE" prompt is actually the DOS prompt. Therefore, the user could type in any DOS command and succeed in, say, wiping out every program in the hard disk.

OK, this may not be likely, but never under-estimate the creativity of neophyte users. When in doubt, they tend to type in anything, and anything may be the wrong thing as far as you and your hard disk are concerned.

The DOS prompt is also notorious for not including any error correction at all. Typing the wrong command can often result in cryptic error messages, at best. DOS also doesn't allow for multiple ways of choosing a program. Only one choice is correct. If you miss, it will still attempt to perform what it thinks you typed in. It has no built-in intelligence.

If you can live with these limitations, the simple method presented here may be the fastest and easiest way to solve the problem.

Below are all the batch files to run the programs represented in the MENULIST above. Type them into the root directory of a hard disk and, in theory, you have a menu system ready to go.

AUTOEXEC.BAT

```
prompt choice$g
echo off
cls
type menulist
```

MENULIST

> ----- > Welcome to Idaho State Library <-----

<W> Microsoft Word
<D> dBase IV
<P> PC-Talk III
<O> OCLC terminal emulation
<L> Lotus 1-2-3
<Q> Quit to DOS

Please enter your choice from the list above
and press [ENTER]

W.BAT

```
CD\WORD
WORD
CD\
AUTOEXEC
```

D.BAT

```
CD\DBASE
DBASE
CD\
AUTOEXEC
```

P.BAT

```
CD\PCTALK
PC-TALK
CD\
AUTOEXEC
```

O.BAT

```
CD\OCLC
OCLC
CD\
AUTOEXEC
```

L.BAT

```
CD\123
123
CD\
AUTOEXEC
```

Q.BAT

```
PROMPT $P$G
CLS
```

## HOW TO WRITE BATCHES

There are at least three ways to write batch files; and we'd better discuss them before we get much further. The first way is through DOS itself. It is only appropriate for tiny batch files that can be written with a line or two and that are not prone to mistakes. This is the Quick and Dirty approach.

At the DOS prompt, shown as "C>" below, type the following (shown in boldface):

```
C>COPY CON:AUTOEXEC.BAT
PROMPT CHOICE$G
ECHO OFF
CLS
TYPE MENULIST
^Z
```

The first line is COPY CON:AUTOEXEC.BAT. This tells DOS to copy what you type at the console (CON) into a file called "AUTOEXEC.BAT" It can be any name you desire, but it must have a ".BAT" extension or it won't work.

The second line establishes the choice prompt. The third line turns off the echo command; and the fourth line clears the screen. The fifth line invokes the DOS command "TYPE" followed by the document you want to appear, called, in this case, "MENULIST".

The sixth line is actually a "Control-Z" not a caret followed by a "Z". Just hold down the "Ctrl" key like a shift key, type the letter "Z", and press [ENTER]. This sequence terminates the batch file and writes it to the disk. You now have a batch file called AUTOEXEC.BAT that looks like this:

```
PROMPT CHOICE$G
ECHO OFF
CLS
TYPE MENULIST
```

When you type "AUTOEXEC" and then hit [ENTER] the batch is invoked. The screen clears, and MENULIST appears on the screen. Because its name is special: AUTOEXEC.BAT, it will also "automatically execute" every time you turn on the computer.

This quick and dirty approach does not require an editor, a word processor, or anything except strong typing skills. The problem with this approach is that you cannot retrieve a line once you type it. That's why accuracy is important. Therefore, it is not appropriate for long, involved batch files that run to several lines. If it's short, go ahead and do it this way. Otherwise, use an editor.

The second way to write batch files is though a program such as Sidekick (published by Borland, International). If you have never encountered Sidekick, a brief explanation is in order.

Sidekick is actually several programs in one. The programs are memory resident, meaning they are stuck in memory at all times, even when you are using another program. You invoke Sidekick through a "hot key" combination, normally by pressing the Control and Alt keys at the same time. Up pops a Sidekick Window which allows you to choose one of several programs. The Sidekick Notepad can be used to write these batch files.

The advantages of Sidekick are several, and of major interest to programmer types. First, once loaded, it's always there lurking in the background, thus eliminating the load-edit-save-quit-reload-try shuffle. Second, Sidekick produces "clean" files that don't have garbage in them. These "straight-ASCII" files have nothing but the letters you type in them. No control codes or strange combinations are present. Therefore, Sidekick files are ideal for writing batch files, which expect this sort of thing. Thirdly, Sidekick files can be quite large (up to 50K) and accommodate the most ambitious batch file. Editing is easy in Sidekick, particularly if you're used to the now archaic Wordstar command set. Fifth, since Sidekick is memory resident, you can try out your batch file attempts immediately. If you're wrong, just re-invoke Sidekick, change the file, save it and try again.

The third way to write batch files is through a full fledged word processor. This means you must invoke the word processor to write the batch files, then quit to get back to the DOS level to try them. The advantage here is that you have the full array of word processing controls available to you. Insofar as that is valuable, it is an asset.

The disadvantage of this approach is that it is a good example of overkill. It can do the job, but it is cumbersome. Many word processors insert control characters within the text file to govern such things as underlining and so on. In order to write a "straight-ASCII" file, special procedures must be invoked. This means quite a few wasted keystrokes and quite a lot of wasted time as you enter and exit the word processor just to write a batch file. Certainly this is preferable compared an attempt to write a large batch file at the DOS prompt, but it pales in comparison to the Sidekick approach.

If it's not obvious, we recommend Sidekick, or its equivalent, as the batch file editor of choice.

# UNIFORM INTERFACE (VERSION TWO)

The second version of the Uniform Interface takes the batch files we have just introduced and makes the entire process a little fancier. The new fancy part is the MENULIST file itself, rather than any of the batches.

In the previous example, the MENULIST file was simply a text file containing the choices available, arranged in a menu-like fashion, with no embellishments. In this example, we add a box around the choices and neaten up the appearance a little bit in order to make the menu appear a little more proper. This can be done in Sidekick, by invoking the box drawing capability built into MS-DOS type computers and accommodated by Sidekick. It can also be done in many word processors, including Microsoft Word and WordPerfect, among others.

With the new MENULIST, you will still have a disguised DOS prompt at the bottom of the screen. Only the menu itself will appear different.

Jake's CD-ROM menu from Idaho State Library is shown on page 31. Notice how neat the entire menu list is, and how the C> prompt will appear immediately below the menu structure itself. Jake didn't change the DOS prompt in this case, but specific directions are given from within the file itself.

The file was written from within WordPerfect and saved as an ASCII file. The box characters are available from within Word-Perfect and are much more complicated than they may seem. The characters that form the edges and intersections are all different. This menu screen, for example, represents ten different "high-ASCII" characters in addition to the text itself. WordPerfect and Microsoft Word will draw these characters and make the intersections work with just a few commands. With Sidekick, at least the older version, you need to look up each character and place it in the text manually. If you need to move fast, you won't have the patience for doing this by hand.

The entire menu box is tabbed over about five spaces so that it appears in the middle of the screen. Each choice has a corresponding batch file on the disk which performs the appropriate action. Read the chapter on CD-ROM for a complete explanation of what Jake is doing with these files. In any event, it is obvious that Jake's menu structure is much more sophisticated than the initial version presented above.

## ASCII AND YOU SHALL RECEIVE

The "high-ASCII" characters deserve a bit of explanation, especially for libraries, which utilize them all the time, perhaps without really knowing. It all relates to a "byte" which just about everybody who has anything to do with computers knows about by now.

A "byte" is composed of eight "bits" or on-off switches. Call them magnetized and demagnetized, present or absent, yin or yang; it doesn't matter. The point is that the switch exists in two states. When we line up the bits side by side, combinations of "on" and "off" represent the different possible characters which you can type on the keyboard. The first 32 or so are control characters which you type by using the CTRL key instead of the shift key. The rest are taken up by the letters of the alphabet, both upper and lower case, numbers, swear symbols, signs, parentheses, etc. As it happens, there is plenty of room within seven bits for all this. Each bit offers two choices, and each time we add a bit to the sequence, we therefore double the number of choices available. Seven bits is two to the seventh power, or 128 possible choices. These first 128 characters are the normal or "low" ASCII characters. But a byte is composed of eight bits. Add the eighth bit and you double the number of choices from 128 to 256. What can you use those other 128 character positions for?

Anything you want. And that's the problem. Everyone has used those second 128 characters for anything they wanted. The first 128 characters are standardized throughout the industry (more or less). The second 128 characters are UP FOR GRABS!

The Epson printer company decided the upper 128 characters (these are the "high-ASCII" characters) would be a good place to stuff italic versions of English characters. IBM decided the high-ASCII characters would be a good place to put lines and symbols, lines that form all sorts of boxes. Ventura Publisher decided this would be a good place to stuff things like copyright symbols. And

Microsoft decided this would be a good place to establish an elaborate substitution scheme for commands in Microsoft Word. This meant that one high-ASCII character could stand for an entire command.

And libraries, bless them, decided the high-ASCII character set would be a good place to stuff Icelandic thorns and Polish "L" characters. That's the standard ALA character set, which no one else in the known world uses. Now the fact is that ALA decided on a standard high-ASCII set long before IBM decided on little boxes, but who do you suppose won that little skirmish? IBM didn't even know there was a skirmish. Where does a Sasquatch sit? Anywhere it wants to.

So how did libraries implement the ALA standard on microcomputers? Both OCLC and WLN, for example, did it by using special video cards with their monitors. These video cards have extra memory on them; and in this extra memory is placed the high-ASCII ALA character set. That way, you can see ALA characters on the screen and on the library customized keyboard of an IBM-type computer. This is also why sometimes, when you run other programs on an OCLC or WLN terminal, the ALA characters appear in places where you would normally expect to find—a box. The ALA character set hasn't been cleared out yet, even though that was maybe supposed to happen. We'll come back to this later because it's going to become even more important in the future.

## MID-LEVEL BATCHING

So far we have shown only elementary examples of batch programs. But it is important to recognize that batches can contain any command you can otherwise issue from the normal DOS prompt. This includes running programs and setting parameters as well as any batch commands that you may be able to use. For example, the batch below sets up a serial port to connect with a mini computer, then runs a program called "LTE" (Library Terminal Emulator) which itself requires information to run correctly.

The first command signs up to the EMULATE directory. The second command is the DOS "MODE" command, that can be used for many things, including setting up the monitor, the serial port, and the parallel port. In this case, it is telling the computer to set up the first serial port (COM1:) at 9600 baud, and to use even parity, seven data bits, and one stop bit. As usual, DOS commands are pretty cryptic. Explanations, such that they are, can be found in the DOS manual. The third command runs LTE and sets it up for seven data bits, one stop bit, and even parity as well. The VUCOM in the line refers to the type of terminal it is supposed to emulate.

```
CD\EMULATE
MODE COM1:9600,E,7,1
LTE WORD=7E1 VUCOM
CD\
AUTOEXEC
```

The fourth command returns to the root directory; and the fifth runs the AUTOEXEC command again to reestablish the menu, a technique seen in even the most elementary batches above. The fourth and fifth lines are executed after you exit from LTE, however that may be done. These last two lines are important because they tidy up what you have done. This is good programming practice. If you change something, change it back before you quit. Clean up after yourself. If you don't do this, you are leaving the computer in an unknown state. The next person who wants to use it may not understand what has been done.

Pay particular attention to any changes in the PATH command. This little beast sets up the search path DOS uses to find programs. If you change it, you may have destroyed the path for a subsequent program. Of course each batch should take care of its own path requirements, but if you're not always in charge of the entire machine, this may be a place to look for possible errors. The point is not to create them for someone else.

If you did not sign back to the root directory, for example, the next command, AUTOEXEC, would probably not work. Why probably? Because if the path were set via DOS, it might find AUTOEXEC, but then AUTOEXEC might not run completely, because the commands are being executed from the wrong directory. Here's how the PATH command works.

PATH works great in theory, but not so great considering the mis-behaving programs that proliferate in the MS-DOS world. The idea is to hook up all the sub-directories of a hard disk together so that the appropriate commands are available anywhere. A simple path command, for example, would be to tie a DOS directory (full of all those rarely-used DOS programs) to everywhere else, like this:

```
PATH C:\DOS
```

With this in place, either by the keyboard or placed in a batch file such as AUTOEXEC.BAT, the DOS commands will be available from any sub-directory. Thus you can format a disk from the directory containing dBase or Lotus 1-2-3 just as if you were in the directory containing the FORMAT.COM program itself. Here's another one:

PATH C:\WORD

This path command ties the WORD directory which contains your WORD processor to any other place on the hard disk. If you do this with Microsoft WORD, for example, you can invoke WORD from the dBase directory, and all the documents you save will reside in the dBase directory. This helps keep documents in their proper places, providing that's where you want them.

This idea also works for sub-directories of sub-directories. Let's say you had a directory for Microsoft Word, and within that directory you had three sub-directories, one for Jeanne, one for Anne, and one for Matthew. This is how the directory tree would look:

```
                                    ————Anne
        C:\(root)———— WORD ————Jeanne
                                    ————Matthew
```

The PATH command would appear in the AUTOEXEC.BAT program as a line just like the one above. This will tie WORD to all the directories. In order for Jeanne to use WORD, you would have her sign up to the JEANNE directory of WORD, then invoke the WORD program. All Jeanne's files would reside in JEANNE and not be confused with similar files, which might also have similar names, in the directory used by MATTHEW. The batch file which did this would include lines such as the following:

```
CD\WORD\JEANNE
WORD
CD\
AUTOEXEC
```

The AUTOEXEC.BAT file would contain separate codes for each of the three people to run "their" copy of WORD. They don't even need to know what's really happening internally. All they know is the code to start up the word processor, different for each of them, probably consisting of only their first names.

The PATH command can be more complicated by stringing various directories together with semi-colons. The following batch strings together the root directory (C:\), the directory for DOS (C:\DOS), the directory holding the Norton Utilities, a very popular commercial utility package (C:\NORTON), and the directory for WORD (C:\WORD). All the programs from any of these directories are "in the path" and available from any other directory.

PATH C:\;C:\DOS;C:\NORTON;C:\WORD

This can create problems. One of the problems is that DOS will search for the program name you type in the current directory first, then in directories in the PATH until it finds the appropriate program. If you have a habit of naming programs the same way in different directories, you could find yourself running the wrong program. We have a habit of naming batches GO.BAT to start up a program. We sign up somewhere, type "GO" and whatever is supposed to happen does, unless we erase the GO.BAT in the current directory, in which case DOS searches for the nearest GO.BAT it can find and runs that instead. As we get deeper into batches, you'll see why the tidying up process is important. It can all get very confusing.

Another problem is that all programs cannot handle these paths. The old Wordstar, for example, has separate pieces of the program residing on the disk (called overlays). You could call up part of Wordstar from a separate directory all right, but when the program reached for an overlay, it looked only in the current directory. Since the overlay was nowhere to be found, the program would crash. Programs these days are supposed to be smarter than that, but you may run into the problem anyway.

This is the major problem with batch files themselves as well. If you don't sign back to the directory that has all the programs called by a batch, then the batch will run, but crash when it fails to find the correct program.

Let's say you did not return to the root directory from the WORD directory and attempted to run the menulist up again. Your buggy batch looks like this:

W.BAT

```
CD\WORD
WORD
AUTOEXEC
```

```
AUTOEXEC.BAT

PROMPT CHOICE$G
ECHO OFF
CLS
TYPE MENULIST
```

The W batch signs up to WORD and runs the program. When you're done with the program, the batch again takes control and runs the AUTOEXEC program. Because the path is set to the root directory with PATH C:\ the AUTOEXEC batch is found and begins to execute. Everything works fine until it gets to the last line, when a "file not found" message appears. Prompt works; ECHO works; and CLS works. Why?

Because MENULIST is in the root directory, but AUTOEXEC is running from the WORD directory. It tries to find MENULIST in WORD, does not, and crashes. The first three lines are internal DOS commands which will work anywhere anytime. They don't require a program to execute because they are part of DOS and, in essence, "memory resident" just like a Sidekick program.

## BATCH CONTROL

The Batch control language for MS-DOS is not much of a language, really. But it has improved over successive releases to the point where it can do a lot more than it could do with release 1.0 of MS-DOS, so many years ago. Up until Release 3.3, for example, DOS batches did not have the ability to call subroutines. Because this may affect how you write batch files, it is discussed below.

If you've done any programming, you know that subroutines are parts of a program that you can call at appropriate times in the execution of a program. If you're writing a data base program which deals with names, for example, you might have a FINDER subroutine which finds names that might already be in the data base. You might call FINDER when you're adding names, changing names, or deleting names. In each case, you can use the same subroutine to actually find the name, then proceed to do what you will with the name once you've found it. Obviously, subroutines mean less coding for you. Once FINDER works, it can be used in any appropriate location just by calling it.

DOS batch files up until release 3.3 could call other batches just fine. They could even call themselves and become "recursive" in the process. But they couldn't use subroutines in the conventional sense. We'll explain why release 3.3 has changed all that below.

But if you have already formatted and loaded your hard disk with DOS 2.1, it is unlikely you are going to remove everything from your hard disk, spend another $100 for DOS 3.3, and reformat the disk just to get this neat feature. Unless you have several hours and a hundred dollars per hard disk, you will live with the old way of doing things.

The basic idea is that a batch file can call another batch file, but that when it does so, the other batch file is in charge of the computer. Like a relay race, the baton does not return to the first batch at all, unless the second batch invokes the first batch intentionally. Here's an example of an AUTOEXEC.BAT passing control to a second batch:

```
AUTOEXEC.BAT

    PATH C:\;C:\WORD
    CD\EMULATE
    GO


GO.BAT

    MODE COM1:9600,7,E,1
    LTE
```

The AUTOEXEC.BAT starts up when the computer is turned on, establishes a path, changes directories to EMULATE, and runs the second batch called GO.BAT. The second batch takes over and does its work. When it's done, it just ends, without passing control anywhere. It could pass control back to AUTOEXEC.BAT, but then AUTOEXEC.BAT would run again, and you'd be in an infinite loop with no way out. You will be able to do this anyway, as will be explained below. The point is that a batch can call another batch, but then the other batch is in charge unless you specifically direct otherwise.

This can all be used to advantage in very complicated set-ups. For example, you could establish an elaborate series of menus in each sub-directory, each of which performed tasks appropriate to the programs in that sub-directory. One of the choices in the sub directory would be to return to the original directory and run the main choices again. Let's look at the very first menu in this chapter again, then create a second batch file to display a sub-menu:

```
-----> Welcome to Idaho State Library <-----

        <W>  Microsoft Word
        <D>  dBase IV
        <P>  PC-Talk III
        <O>  OCLC terminal emulation
        <L>  Lotus 1-2-3
        <Q>  Quit to DOS

Please enter your choice from the list above
and press [ENTER]
```

1)  W.BAT

    ```
    CD\WORD
    CLS
    TYPE WORDLIST
    ```

2)  WORDLIST

    ```
    -----> Welcome to The WORD Sub-Menu <-----

            <W>  Microsoft Word
            <F>  Format a disk
            <B>  Backup all documents to Drive a:
            <R>  Return to Main Menu
    ```

3)  R.BAT

    ```
    CD\
    AUTOEXEC
    ```

Assume that W.BAT was called by the user from the original menu. Instead of running a program directly, it runs a second menu list, from which the user makes a second choice. The SECOND W.BAT in the WORD sub-directory would run WORD, then re-run the SECOND menu list when WORD was finished. The user must type the <R> choice before returning to the root directory and the Main Menu from which all this started. Choices <F> and <B> would run the FORMAT.COM program and prompt the user to place a disk in drive A: before copying all *.DOC files to the disk, respectively. We have not repeated those batches here.

These sub-menus and quite a few programs can all be handled quite nicely by using batch files and avoiding subroutines altogether. It works.

## BATCHES WITH CHOICES

Batches are great for stringing commands together. We've shown how you can use elementary and mid-level batches above. In this manner, separate batches can be written to control each choice made by the user. When the batch is done, it calls an original batch which gives the user the same choices again. This all works, and there is no reason you can't use it. No one said it had to be elegant, or that the next programmer down the line had to understand what you have set up.

However, there are ways to use batch files so that much of the process resides within one file instead of several. Choices can be made from within a single batch file. To do so requires a separate program or two. One of them is the ASK program available in the Norton Utilities.

The Norton Utilities is a set of programs sold by Peter Norton which allows an MS-DOS computer user to perform tasks otherwise difficult. In the Advanced edition there are twenty-four programs that do small things like beep the speaker, or do large things like recover accidentally erased files. More than a few people have paid for the Norton Utilities by being able to recover an accidentally erased file on a disk.

The ASK Utility is a very small program that allows a user to type a choice from within a batch file and have that choice picked up by the batch and used to execute different programs. In order to use it, you must also use the ability of batch files to "branch" within the batch. Assume the same menulist presented in the first part of this chapter. Below is an incomplete batch file, representing the first part of this process.

```
prompt choice$g
echo off
cls
type menulist
ask "Which choice? ",wdpolq
if errorlevel 6 goto quit
if errorlevel 5 goto lotus
if errorlevel 4 goto oclc
if errorlevel 3 goto pctalk
if errorlevel 2 goto dbase
if errorlevel 1 goto word
sub routines go here
```

What's happened so far? The DOS prompt has been replaced by Norton's ASK command. The prompt follows the word "Ask," then a comma, then the acceptable choices corresponding to the choices presented by the menulist file. ASK sets what is called an ERRORLEVEL in DOS. The highest error level is assigned to the last choice in the list. There are six choices; therefore "q", the sixth choice in the list, gets error level 6. Lotus 1-2-3 gets error level 5, and so on. DOS checks the error levels highest first, so the IF commands must also be in that order.

(Important Note: Beginning with Version 4.5 of Norton, the correct syntax for ASK is "BE ASK" because the ASK command has been included within a more general BATCH ENHANCE-MENT program. It still works the same way.)

The IF command is coupled with the GOTO command, which you haven't seen yet. It refers to a label in the batch file. Anything beyond that label gets executed, including other labels. Below is the label for word, and its subsequent commands:

```
:word
cd word
word
cd\
autoexec
```

Look familiar? It should because it is exactly the same small batch file that was once called W.BAT. Now it resides within the AUTOEXEC.BAT file; when it is all done with running WORD, the batch calls itself, and the main menu displays once again.

Now you can see how a recursive batch will work without getting you into an infinite loop. If you can pick choices from within the batch, then the number of files can be reduced drastically. Everything can be controlled by a single batch file. Notice also that the last line within the subroutine takes you out of that subroutine. Ensure you always do this. If you don't, the batch will fall right through to the next subroutine:

```
:word
cd word
word
cd\
:lotus [mistake]
cd 123
123
cd\
```

In the case above, for example, after finishing the WORD program, the batch again takes charge, signs down to the root directory, then immediately executes the lotus subroutine, the next command in the file. If you want to get a little fancier, the last line could be a call to a beginning label within the batch. This would prevent the batch from starting over at the beginning. It is useful if the beginning of your AUTOEXEC batch, in particular, does other things before it displays the menu.

The ASK command is the tool which makes all this manipulation within a batch possible. It is not the only program that can do this, as you shall see, but it is one that is readily available.

The ASK command will accept both upper and lower case letters corresponding to the ones you type in the acceptable list beyond the quote marks in the command itself. It will not accept any other command, but only beeps at the user. This is a clear advantage over the raw DOS prompt which will attempt to invoke anything typed. ASK prevents unauthorized choices, though perhaps not too elegantly. The user is forced into choosing one of the commands for which you provide.

The flip side to using the ASK command is that it forces you to learn more batch commands and to keep one big batch file all straight. Yet some of the disadvantages of batches still prevail. If you call another batch from within this big batch, for example, control still passes to that second batch. Control will not pass back to this batch unless you force the return by invoking it in the second batch file.

## CALL

The Call command was implemented in MS-DOS 3.3, finally. CALL allows you to call other batches. When the other batch ends, control is returned to the calling batch. It's a great feature if you have it; it does not exist in DOS versions prior to 3.3. If all your computers have DOS 3.3 or above, you may want to incorporate CALL into your batches. If not, the older batches without CALL will still work just fine. Many of our own computers are still running DOS 2.1, so we do not normally include the CALL command in our own batches. We write for the lowest common denominator in our system in order for the batches to be widely acceptable over the organization without undue modification.

```
AUTOEXEC.BAT

ECHO OFF
PATH C:\;C:\WORD
TYPE MENULIST
```

```
ASK "Which Choice? ",QE
IF ERRORLEVEL 2 GOTO EMULATE
IF ERRORLEVEL 1 GOTO QUIT
:EMULATE
CD\EMULATE
CALL GO
AUTOEXEC
:QUIT
CD\
ECHO ON
```

GO.BAT

```
MODE COM1:9600,7,E,1
```

Above are the same two batches as introduced earlier in this chapter. This time, AUTOEXEC calls the GO.BAT, which still signs back to the root directory before ending. When it does, control is returned to the original batch, and AUTOEXEC is again executed. This is yet another added feature that makes batch commands closer to a real programming language. Only a very liberal definition would grant batch commands this status, but at least it has more programming features than it once did; and they are useful.

# UNIFORM INTERFACE (THIRD VERSION)

The first version of the Uniform Interface does the required tasks with little fanfare. The second version adds the concept of error correction as well as batches that can be more or less self contained. Even though it is an improvement, it isn't all that sophisticated. It simply does not meet contemporary standards for a "user-friendly" interface.

"User friendly" is a hackneyed term that has probably lost most of its original meaning. To people who love graphical interfaces such as found on the Apple Macintosh, the phrase only applies if you delete files by placing them in a garbage can with a mouse. Any English phrasing is verboten; and a DOS prompt is greeted with absolute horror.

We have seen people who are so convinced garbage can interfacing is the answer that they have blinded themselves to other alternatives available. However, this attitude may not be based so much on a comparison of alternatives, but instead be a result of an introduction to computers using one interface over another. Once they have seen what wonderful things computers can do, they attribute this to the interface of the particular machine, failing to generalize. The same is true of software packages as well.

Computer makers know this, of course, and this is why they fight it out in the educational marketplace by offering substantial discounts to schools and teachers. Once students learn Apple, they will think Apple is great. They will recommend Apple for purchase. IBM does the same thing in colleges and universities. If the computer science majors learn IBM equipment, who do you think has the best shot at selling mainframe computers in the corporate world?

In the MS-DOS world "Windows" and the new "Presentation Manager" are attempts to answer the DOS prompt criticism. However, they aren't the first programs attempting to insulate the users from knowing how to work the system. Desqview is a DOS-shell that does the same thing, along with some other important things such as allowing a computer to run more than one program at once. Other "shell" programs such as 1Dir+ and Norton's Commander attempt to do the same thing.

Windows-type interfaces may very well take over in the future. Certainly IBM is now headed in that direction. As that happens, we will all need to spend another few dollars to attach a Mouse to our current computer so that we might pull down Windows and throw files in the garbage can. Until that happens, we're stuck with alternative interfaces.

Probably the most common "interface" in the MS-DOS world is the "point and shoot" bar menu popularized by such programs as Lotus 1-2-3 and the Microsoft array of products, including Microsoft Word. The idea here is place choices on a menu and cover them with a moving light bar, which is just a big cursor covering several characters instead of just one. The user moves the light bar to cover the appropriate menu choice with the arrow keys, then presses the [Enter] key to invoke that choice. Alternatively, the user can type the first letter of the first word of the choice, and the program will also be invoked.

Other characteristics of this moving bar structure include error correction and the ability to back out of the structure with the [ESCAPE] key. If the user types a choice which is not invoked by the moving bar, the menu just sits there waiting for the correct answer. In this sense, it isn't much different than the ASK command discussed above. The important point is that the feature exists. Backing out of a menu with [ESCAPE] allows the user a standard way to reverse operations. In theory, a cascading series of moving bar menus can be attached to any series of applications. Moving bar menus also always have a choice which returns to the previous menu or lets the user out of the menu application altogether.

Until recently, programming a moving bar menu structure was reserved for true experts, the ones whose minds are wired in hexadecimal code and can handle these sorts of things. However, several utilities are now on the market which allow a normal person to construct moving bar menus easily and efficiently. No particular expertise is needed, though we don't claim an absolute novice will be able to instantly pick up the procedures. Familiarity with computers always helps.

Our favorite such program is an inexpensive one called "Saywhat?!" published by The Research Group (88 South Linden Ave., South San Francisco, CA 94080). It costs a whopping $49.95. It's amazing how much it can do for the price.

The basic idea behind Saywhat?! is screen generation. As we have previously discussed, drawing boxes with a PC is problematical at best. Some word processors allow boxes to be drawn on the screen, but that's where the facility stops. Saywhat?! is intended to be used by programmers who want to add screens to their applications. For programmers, drawing screens is not exactly hard—the techniques are well known. But drawing screens is incredibly tedious work. It is work complicated when a programmer wants to display information at particular places on the screen using "X-Y" coordinates. One character off and the entire screen is off, requiring repeated attempts at success.

Saywhat?! has changed all that by allowing a programmer to "paint" a screen using commands in Saywhat?! Using very simple commands, Saywhat?! allows boxes to be drawn anywhere. Any part of the screen can be filled with any "attribute" of color or brightness. Creative types can even use the high-ASCII set to draw pictures and illustrations. These will never be shown in the Louvre, but they do add a dimension, however slim, to the programming process.

The programmer specifies where variables are to show up on the screen. Saywhat?! takes note of these placements, then writes a short program in the language of choice to do so. The programmer can then take the program segment and incorporate it into the program at hand, thus skipping the tedious work of drawing and placing screens by hand. The program is written in the language of choice, including BASIC, Pascal, dBase, and C. Instructions for incorporating these screens within other languages are also provided.

But that's not all. Saywhat?! saves the screen to disk as a single file that can be called up from within the program. Utilities provided with Saywhat?! allow the screens to pop up on the screen instantly. There aren't any delays to watch the screen fill up; the screens just appear immediately. Because of an internal paging scheme, these screens can pop up on top of one another. Sub-screens with further choices pop on top of full screens, and back down again. The entire process is quite wondrous to behold.

Beginning with version 3.6 Saywhat?! also does moving bar menus. The programmer (that's you) constructs a screen in Saywhat, then establishes the menu choices. They can be within a box or not, as preferred. A single command (Alt-B) establishes the corners of the moving bars. They are constructed and saved with the screen itself. When the screen is popped into an application, the moving bar works just like in a real program, just like in Lotus 1-2-3 or Microsoft Word. The bar moves with the arrow keys. [Enter] or the first letter selects the choice. The programmer traps the choice and executes the program depending on the results.

How does the programmer trap the choice? Exactly like we just did above using Norton's ASK command. Saywhat?! works with batch files. Below is an example of a Saywhat program compared to version Two of the Uniform Interface, described above.

*With Saywhat?!*

```
AUTOEXEC.BAT
    ECHO OFF
    PATH C:\;C:\WORD
    VIDPOP
    POP MENULIST
    SETERROR
    IF ERRORLEVEL 2 GOTO EMULATE
    IF ERRORLEVEL 1 GOTO QUIT
    :EMULATE
    CD\EMULATE
    LTE
    CD\
    AUTOEXEC
    :QUIT
    CD\
    ECHO ON
```

*With Norton's ASK*

```
AUTOEXEC.BAT
    ECHO OFF
    PATH C:\;C:\WORD
    TYPE MENULIST
    ASK "Which Choice? ",QE
    IF ERRORLEVEL 2 GOTO EMULATE
    IF ERRORLEVEL 1 GOTO QUIT
    :EMULATE
    CD\EMULATE
    LTE
    CD\
    AUTOEXEC
    :QUIT
    CD\
    ECHO ON
```

The differences between these two batches are minimal. Three additional programs are required to be on the disk: VIDPOP, POP, and SETERROR. These all come with Saywhat?! and can be freely included in your applications.

VIDPOP is a memory resident program that governs the screens generated by Saywhat?! It sits up in memory and waits for a screen to be generated. In our experience, it rarely interferes with other programs that may run from the batch files. We freely use it with our online bibliographic utility with no ill effects. It also works with dBase IV, one of the most memory hungry programs we've encountered. Obviously, we can't ensure that every program in the world will run perfectly with VIDPOP in place, but it certainly has not proven a problem with us. VIDPOP needs to be invoked only once at the top of a batch, then never again until you kill it intentionally or start up the computer again.

POP is a small program that actually pops Saywhat?! screens. It is invoked as you see here, with the name of the screen following the program name. Instead of TYPE MENULIST, you POP MENULIST.

SETERROR must be invoked as you see here before popping the screen. It does what its name suggests, sets up the error levels to be trapped by the program. The error levels work exactly like in the Norton version, high error level first, in order. Once trapped, you can do what you will with the resulting information.

Writing screens with Saywhat is not any more work than writing screens in a word processor, therefore the work is approximately the same. The MENULIST file still must be created somehow. With Saywhat, of course, many more options are available to you.

The Saywhat approach has several advantages. The error correction is superb. The user must use the choices available, and no others will work. The moving bar menus are as close to a standard user interface as we have in MS-DOS. If a user is familiar with any one of a number of applications, using a menu in Saywhat will be intuitive and easy. There's simply not that much to it. The interface itself looks very professional. Indeed, until recently only professionals could write menu structures like this. Saywhat has brought this facility to the rest of us. If you program at all, your life will be much easier. If you use Saywhat in the manner described, life will be easier for your users as well.

# 3 APPLICATIONS TOOLBOX

In any organization that has more than just one PC, there will be someone who is supposed to know how these things work. If you are reading this, chances are you are that person, or are about to become one. This means your job is just a little different than the job of the users you are there to serve. The job gets mixed reviews. On the one hand, you have become the Computer Guru who can fix anything. A user will run breathless to your desk to report a misbehaving printer. Somehow, it's spewing paper all over the floor. What can you do?

You arrive at the disaster area, sniff around the printer a little while, then turn it off and back on again, thus clearing any control codes which may have affected its operation, and also completely clearing the buffer. Suddenly, the printer works properly.

"Oh, my goodness, what did you do?"

"Well, I had to drain the buffer overflow valve which was interfering with the applications interface register. It's OK now. Call me if you have any more problems."

Thus legends are born. Sometimes you even don't know what caused a problem. The trick is to fix it anyway. It may be embarrassing to encounter this, since you know the reason you are the Guru is because you first encountered the same problem twenty minutes ago, or because you have a six-month lead on the other employees in the office.

Granted, not all problems can be cleared up this easily. But over the course of a few seasons, you will begin to assemble a bag of tricks to help you decipher the runes and utter the appropriate incantations. This is your half of the Applications Toolbox, which we'll talk about first. The other half will consist of the software used by your organization. In both cases, the tools consist of software programs as opposed to hammers and screwdrivers, which are covered in Chapter 9.

## APPLICATIONS TOOLBOX (GURU VERSION)

The Applications Toolbox (Guru Version) consists of software tools which you can use to diagnose problems, effect data transfers from one format to another, and generally help keep your act together. What we recommend here are not the only tools available. Indeed, some of your tools will depend specifically on what hardware you have installed. But we have grown to know and love the ones we do use, and we maintain they do the job as stated. If you have a favorite tool by another manufacturer that you find adequate, or even superior, great! Please let us know so we can try it, too.

We are not attempting to capture information on every neat program ever hacked which does something useful. Our tolerance for such utilities is extremely low. If it doesn't grab our attention in about ten seconds, it's gone. Many of the public domain utilities are of this nature. They do something neat; and they may represent a feat of programming expertise. Many times, however, the same sort of thing has been done more elegantly in a commercial program. Disk sector readers, for example, abound on the public bulletin boards. That's great, but the Norton Utilities, Advanced Edition provides everything you'd ever need in a sector editor. Why bother with yet another one? It's a waste of time.

These tools are listed with a view to helping others. That is, we're not attempting to put together a toolbox just for you to use on your own machine. That would cover different priorities. The memory resident utilities you would use as an individual may be totally inappropriate to install on every PC in the place. They are appropriate if you have an entire fleet of PCs to manage.

Below, the list price and publisher are given in parentheses. The "street price" is given following list price. This is the price you can expect to pay for the package if you can avail yourself of mail order. 40% discounts off list are common; 50% is possible. We're resigned to the fact we will probably be caught with wrong prices by the time this sees print. Unless someone gets very greedy, they should be similar.

## NORTON

($150.00/$89.00: Peter Norton) Probably the most famous software tool in general use, judging by its stellar sales history, is The Norton Utilities. It has gone through several revisions, the latest of which is the Advanced Edition. Sold alongside the Advanced Edition is Norton 4.5. Though cheaper, it does not have a few of the useful utilities included in the more expensive edition. His newest releases are much more user-friendly than earlier versions. At this point, most of them work on automatic pilot. They are all particularly useful in management of a hard disk. And what kind of interface do you think the package has? Moving bar, of course. The Advanced Utilities include all of the following:

**ASK** we've covered in depth in Chapter Two, now a part of the Batch Enhance program.

**BEEP** beeps the speaker. This may not sound like much, but you could use it within a batch file to warn the user to perform some task. Through options, you can beep the speaker at certain frequencies and for varied times. You could even construct little tunes, just like the home drier playing "How Dry I Am" at the end of a cycle.

In the latest edition of Norton, both ASK and BEEP have been stored in the Batch Enhancer program, along with several other minor utilities. The method of invoking them is slightly different, but they accomplish the same tasks as before.

**DIRECTORY SORT (DS)** sorts directories of any disk by name, extension, time, date, or even size. That way, the directory entries can be in any order you specify. This is particularly useful on a hard disk where you may want to keep all the directories in one place. Typing "DS EN" for example will sort the root directory by extension, then by name. This results in all the sub-directories appearing at the top of the directory in alphabetical order before files appear below. If you work with a great many hard disks, this utility can help you keep the disks in order and familiar. It makes things easier.

You can also sort by date, useful for clearing old files. Since DS is so fast and easy, you can sort any way you want to just for a moment, then back to your preferred order.

**DISK TEST (DT)** allows you to check a disk for errors. When a disk is formatted at a low level at the factory, it undergoes a series of tests that point out bad places on the disk. Again, when the disk is formatted by DOS, bad sectors are flagged and made unavailable to hold programs. Unfortunately, errors don't stop happening after installation. This program checks the disk for new errors and flags them appropriately.

**FILE ATTRIBUTES (FA)** allows you to change attributes of a file. DOS can set attributes of a file to things like READ ONLY or HIDDEN. If you are trying to hide files from users, this may be a way to do it. We don't recommend it, but the utility is available if needed.

**FILE FIND (FF)** finds files, surprise. To floppy-only users this may seem sort of silly, but on hard disks full of sub-directories, this utility could be useful. You know that file is on the disk somewhere, but where? FF will tell you.

**FILE INFO (FI)** is a fancy directory command which allows you to attach comments to file names.

**FORMAT RECOVER (FR)** is extremely useful in case you

accidentally format a hard disk. When you do format a disk, you are not erasing everything on it. Instead, you are simply setting up signs and roads as if the disk were a new subdivision. Format Recover allows you to recover much of what was on the disk. It may not be entirely successful, but it's worth a try if you find yourself in this unfortunate predicament. We know you would never do this, but perhaps one of your users might. And it will be up to you to recover.

**FILE SIZE (FS)** tells you the size of the files, really. The byte information in a directory information is actually wrong. It may show you the number of bytes in a file, but it doesn't tell you how much space a file takes up. In DOS 2.1, for example, each file takes a minimum size of 8192 bytes, even if the number of bytes shown in the directory entry is only two. A file taking up 8190 bytes also takes up 8192 bytes, really. That's the minimum size. Knowing this information can help you, particularly if file space is getting tight. FS will tell you the real size, and also how much of this space is slack space that is being wasted.

**LIST DIRECTORIES (LD)** may be useful to you. It just lists the directories, one after the other. DOS has a similar command itself.

**LINE PRINT (LP)** is a truly useful program for documenting your programming. It allows you to specify any file or group of files to print, either to a file, the screen, or a printer, complete with line numbers, date printed, page numbers, etc. It is similar to the DOS TYPE command, except much more sophisticated. Any program you write, including batch files, should be documented and printed somewhere. LP does the job well with a minimum of bother.

**NORTON CHANGE DIRECTORY (NCD)** is a fancy form of the DOS CHDIR (CD) command. With Norton's version, you needn't specify the entire directory name. We judge this of marginal usefulness.

**NORTON UTILITY (NU)** is the heart of the Norton system of utilities. It allows you to read and write to any file or any space on the disk. It allows you to get at the innards of files to see what they are really made of. It answers the question, "OK, What did they do this time, really?" with no guesswork.

For example, let's say you are hooked to an online utility which downloads records to you. It also prints reports, but the reports aren't what you would like. Yet you know there is more information in the downloaded file than what is printing out. Your task, should you decide to accept it, is to get in that file and find out how "they" put it together so you can take it apart again and load the information into your own data base management system. Then you can produce reports the way you want them.

NU allows you to see the structure of a file in ASCII, or hexadecimal codes. You can then tell specifically if the file contains carriage returns, line feeds, both, or neither at the end of a record. You can tell if they have placed a strange delimiter in the file. You can discover exactly what is there.

Not only can you find what is there, you can also change it, via hexadecimal codes, to exactly what you want to appear. And you can also piece together fragmented files that have been destroyed because you erased them accidentally.

The more advanced a user you are, the more the NU utility will do for you. It is very powerful, allowing you to mess with file allocation tables and other areas that will absolutely destroy your hard disk if you don't know what you're doing. Still, Norton Utilities would be worth the price if this the only program that was included.

**QUICK UNERASE (QU)** This program is also worth the price of the utilities just by itself. As its name implies, this program can find and restore files you may have erased by mistake. It is very easy to use. Don't say it will never happen to you. We once were erasing files on a floppy and accidentally erased all the files on the root directory of our hard disk. It's just that the C> prompt got on the screen instead of the A> prompt. When it asked, "Are you sure? (Y/N)" we typed "Y" accidentally, a bad move.

Instead of committing hari kari, we just swore mildly, hauled out QU, and un-erased all the files we had just clobbered. It took about thirty seconds. That's because when DOS erases a file, it doesn't really erase it. It just pretends to. Instead, it erases the first letter of the file name, and that's all. This releases the sector formerly in use by that file for use by the next file you save. If you can restore that one character back to normal BEFORE YOU SAVE ANOTHER FILE, chances are you can fully recover that file. That's what Quick Unerase is all about; and it works well. It's not as sophisticated as the unerase routines in the NU program itself, but it trades off sophistication with speed of use. If you're moving fast, it won't even slow you down.

**SCREEN ATTRIBUTES (SA)** allows you to change screen appearances including color, brightness, and blinking. There are other utilities that can do this as well. We judge this program to be a mild addition to the package.

**SPEED DISK (SD)** is available in the Advanced Utilities only. After a hard disk has been in use for awhile, the files have been saved and erased many times. As explained earlier, an erased file just frees up its once-used sectors for use by another file. Unless the second file is exactly the same size as the first file, it will use part of or more than the space the original file used. This means the second file becomes fragmented. Part of the file is on one place on the disk; another part is somewhere else. Eventually this would be like reading a book with one page on one table and another page on another table, perhaps in another room. It slows the disk considerably.

The task of Speed Disk is to rewrite all the files so that they have clusters that are next to one another. We have used this more than once. For disks that have little fragmentation, there is really no difference. But for disks that are subject to fragmentation, this re-write of the files has a perceptible effect. Considering that hard disks are pretty fast anyway, the fact that a human being can see and feel this difference in the way the disk operates shows how effective it is.

**SYSTEM INFORMATION (SI)** This is a famous Norton Utility because the results of its tests are used by computer manufacturers to prove they have fast machines. One of the tests of SI is a measurement of speed. An SI rating of 1.0 means that a computer runs at a speed equivalent to an IBM PC running at 4.77 MHz using an 8088 microprocessor. An SI rating of 2.0 means the computer is running twice as fast.

Many clones of PCs, often called "Turbo PCs" which are made overseas have a clock speed of about 8MHz instead of the original 4.77. This boosts the performance to about 1.7. IBM AT computers run at about 5.0 normally. This is because they use a much faster microprocessor called an 80286. It works more efficiently than an 8088, and it runs at a faster clock speed as well.

Other manufacturers have been able to boost their 80286 PCs to run at an SI of at least 10.0. In other words, it runs at ten times the speed of an old 4.77 MHz PC. Now we're getting into some significant speed increases. The newest PCs running with the 80386 processor at speeds in excess of 25 MHz have clocked SI ratings close to 30.0.

This entire concept has been severely criticized. Responding to this criticism, Norton revised the index to also include a measurement of disk speed. No matter how fast the CPU in a computer runs, it won't have much effect on output from a hard disk. The combination of a fast processor coupled with a slow hard disk is like a race car pulling a house trailer. It is simply not going to perform as effectively.

Another criticism of the SI index is that it is weighted by certain esoteric reasons to favor one type of processing over another. The technical details don't matter much here. The criticism is much like that of EPA mileage estimates in that the index does not measure they types of processing typically encountered in the real world.

A third criticism of the speed index is that both software and hardware manufacturers have been accused of optimizing their product to perform well in such a test. It is possible for such a manufacturer to include in their machine a "Norton Detector" that looks for a speed check program like Norton's, then conveniently shortcuts the program and fools it into thinking the machine is running much faster than it really is.

PC Tools also has a speed index, expressed as a percentage. An AT clone running at 10.0 on Norton rates at about 475% on PC Tools.

Is all this really important? Yes, it is. Even though a roundly heard criticism of fast computers is, "How fast does a word processor need to be?" the fact is that a fast computer is easier to use than a slow computer. The screen displays in a word processor do scroll much faster than they would under a slower machine. This is particularly true of graphics-based systems such as Microsoft Word and Windows. It is also true of CAD (Computer Aided Design) systems, graphics, and data base systems. The difference in speed in writing indexes, for example, may allow a programmer to write a better data base program with fewer steps. On slower computers, the programmer may choose a separate processing step because updating indexes as they are changed would take too long. By eliminating this step in a faster computer, the program becomes easier to use.

Programs such as Ventura Publisher and Pagemaker are used for desktop publishing. They will hardly run on slower PCs. Because their operations are so heavily graphics oriented, they virtually require fast computers. As we move further toward graphics-based user interfaces, this issue will become more acute. Don't let anyone tell you speed is not a factor. Faster is better, not because of the speed itself, but because of the opportunities which unfold to take advantage of it.

Although the discussion of SI always revolves around the index number itself, SI provides quite a lot of other useful information as well. SI can tell what version of DOS is installed on a machine. If you don't know and haven't memorized how large a COMMAND.COM file of a particular version of DOS is, you won't know just by looking. SI searches the computer for the date and name on the ROM BIOS, an important part of the internal coding which has implications for what hardware and software will run on a system. It tells you how much memory is installed in the computer, how many disk drives, serial and parallel ports, and what type of microprocessor or co-processor is installed. SI is useful for more than speed.

**TIME MARK (TM)** is a useful little utility that writes the time and date on the screen or to a disk file. It also keeps track of time so that you can tell for how long a given task has been performed. We use the TM utility to keep a complete log on disk of every time we use a computer. TM is part of the AUTOEXEC.BAT file that starts the computer. It marks the time to a file. When we are done, we run another batch, called STOP.BAT, which combines with the start time, computes the elapsed time, and writes the combined information to a log. This is unique to Norton.

**TEXT SEARCH (TS)** allows you to search for a string of text that is in a file somewhere. Let's say you are programming and decide you need to change the name of a subroutine which is a separate file called by several different programs. Which programs have called your subroutine? Use TS to find them by supplying the name of the subroutine and allowing the program to search through all the files, listing each occurrence. This could also be useful when one of your users can't find the one file on Geoduck Public Library on the hard disk. TS will take care of them in short order.

**UNREMOVE DIRECTORY (UD)** is the same sort of utility as Unerase, except this time you're dealing with directory entries. You would use it if you decided you had erased not only the files, but an entire sub-directory by mistake. IF YOU HAD DONE NOTHING SINCE YOUR MISTAKE using UD is as simple as using QU. The files have a slightly different structure technically, so another program is necessary.

**VOLUME LABEL (VL)** allows you to change the volume label of a disk., We don't know any real people who use volume labels. If you do or know someone who does, please let us know. And let us know why, too.

**WIPEDISK and WIPEFILE.** Watch out with these, Wipefile doesn't just erase the first character of a file name, it overwrites every character in a file with the character you specify. In other words, it totally erases it. Can you think of a good reason to use Wipefile? How about Wipedisk? But if you're paranoid about security, or work for the government, perhaps these will be useful to you. If only Ollie North had understood how to erase files, we would not have had an entire Fall of entertainment on network TV.

We have detailed the many utilities within Norton to show you the breadth of tools it provides. With the utilities that follow, we will detail those tools that are significantly different from Norton, or ones that simply don't exist in Norton at all. Please see the table on page 65 for a side-by-side comparison of the ones we have detailed.

## SIDEKICK

($84.95/$44.00: Borland International) According to legend, Sidekick was produced in-house by Borland, International, for use by their programmers in writing other applications. Industry gossip columnists insist this is not true and that Sidekick was developed as a commercial product from the beginning. Whatever its true origins, Sidekick, and now Sidekick Plus, have earned for their publishers a deserved place in microcomputer software.

Sidekick is a series of memory-resident utilities that are helpful in any attempt at managing PCs. Sidekick (the original) provides five basic utilities, all available from a single keystroke while running other programs.

The Notepad may be the most useful utility of all. As discussed in Chapter Two, it allows you to write programs, batches, notes, or anything else typed at the keyboard in a file from 4K to 48K as you are working. This is an excellent way to write batch files, or to capture screen data when you are writing documentation. The notepad can both import information from the screen into the notepad, or export data from the notepad into the program you are working on.

A Calculator is also part of this package. It looks like a normal four function calculator that appears on the screen. One added advantage is that it can transform any number input from decimal to hexadecimal or binary and back the other way. If for some reason you need hex codes, the calculator can provide them.

The Calendar's purpose in life is to keep your appointments. Nice idea, but we're not convinced it is the most useful part of this package. We feel the same way about the Dialer, which will dial telephone numbers for you. You'd need to be a truly dedicated Sidekick user to have it dial the phone.

The ASCII table is useful. It allows you to look up the ASCII code for any character in the set of 256 possible codes. For characters up to ASCII 31 it provides the name (mnemonic) of the character, the Control code used to produce it, what it looks like on the screen, and both the hexadecimal and decimal equivalents. For characters above this low range, it provides the character, plus both its decimal and hexadecimal equivalents.

We consider the Notepad to be an indispensable tool for the local Guru. The ASCII table and calculator are also useful. The last two packages we could do without. Oh, yes. It uses a moving bar interface.

## MEMORY DIAGNOSTICS

One of the more difficult aspects of dealing with PCs is that chips fail. Unfortunately, they don't just fail completely. Instead, they fail intermittently for quite some time before they fail completely enough to keep the computer from working. We've had computer memory chips fail in such a way that the answers to spreadsheet formulas were calculated incorrectly without slowing down the computer. Other times the program running behaved erratically, but only under certain operations that happened to be handled by parts of the program which were housed at that memory location.

We've used a number of memory test utilities. If you have an expansion card installed, memory check utilities are usually included. Our favorite is a memory test program from Quadram Corporation for use on their Quadboard expansion card. It lights up pictures of memory chips on the screen when they are bad. It is a simple matter to pull the errant chip and replace it with a good one. Other memory diagnostics are more cryptic, ending in the internal error codes supplied by IBM. Any 2000 error is a memory error. The number associated with this error will tell you which chip is bad, but only if you have the proper documentation to allow you to translate.

Unfortunately, a memory test program for one board will not work on the board produced by another manufacturer. We've tried Quadram's nifty utility on other boards. Sadly, it doesn't work. If you install a particular after-market expansion memory board, you're probably stuck with the test utility that comes with that board.

## PC TOOLS

($150.00/$79.00: Central Point Software) PC Tools is another very comprehensive set of utilities much like the Norton Utilities. Its basic difference from Norton is that most of the utilities are (or can be) memory resident. Just like Sidekick, the utilities can be run from within other programs. PC Tools also has more utilities than Norton. In some respects it is a hybrid between the first two programs.

PC Tools lacks only a few of the Norton Utilities. The batch commands ASK and BEEP are absent, as are TIMEMARK, WIPEDISK, WIPEFILE, and a screen attribute change utility. We judge both ASK and the timemark utility useful; they are a loss with PC Tools. But certainly PC Tools more than makes up for this loss with the additional facilities available.

A major addition is a complete backup system, run as a separate utility outside the normal program. It works very much like FASTBACK in speed and ease of use. Files are backed up onto floppy disks; and, of course, they can be restored. To backup 15 megabytes of data onto 12 1.2MB disks takes 15 minutes the first time, and seven minutes of the disks are already formatted. The formatting is special; and you can't read these disks normally. Instead, PC Tools' own restore program must be used in this process. After a full backup has been done, incremental backups are very fast. It can take just a few seconds, quite literally, to back up changed files at the end of the day.

From a cost standpoint, this one utility included with PC Tools is virtually free. Fastback, a very similar competitor, costs $189, or about $110 mail order, and that's all it does. At $150.00 retail and $77.00 or so mail order, PC Tools provides excellent value for this program alone. It was once much cheaper than this, but the latest revision boosted the price considerably.

In our original testing PC Tools backup was about 35% faster than Fastback, but we suspect this is temporary as Fastback came out with a new release, then Central Point did the same thing. This will turn out very much like Microsoft Word versus WordPerfect. First one supports a feature, then the other does. The leadership bounces back and forth, just like a tight basketball game.

But PC Tools doesn't stop there. Through the use of a MIRROR program, PC Tools actually keeps track of a hard disk's file allocation table (FAT). This table is a complete record of where on the disk all files are located. If this table is destroyed, recovering from a system crash is well nigh impossible. DOS keeps two copies of this table on each hard disk. Unfortunately, they are right next to each other, the software equivalent of keeping all your eggs in one basket. The statistical probability of a crash getting both tables at once is higher than it should be. The MIRROR program alleviates this liability. PC Tools uses the file made by MIRROR in the recovery process, should both FAT directories be destroyed.

PC Tools also has a cache program. This can help programs execute faster, particularly when they involve many reads to a disk. By placing the most often used disk sectors in memory, the programs work faster. This is exactly the same technique used on RAM disks and PC speed up boards.

PC Tools' word processing program is much like Sidekick's. It is memory resident, and it pops up on command. However, it is not anywhere near as versatile as its Sidekick counterpart. You cannot import screen text into the word processor, or take part of the text and paste it into another program. We feel these two features are what makes Sidekick's word processor really functional. The lack of them in PC Tools means that part of its utilities is not as worthwhile as they would have you believe.

Many of the utilities in PC Tools act as replacements for typical DOS commands. They have their own copy and format commands, for example, which have little differences that are supposed to improve them. Indeed, PC Tools acts very much like a DOS shell wrapping around the entire DOS command structure. You could probably survive by never running another DOS command, but only using PC Tools. Unlike most DOS shells, PC Tools does not allow you to RUN programs from within the shell. This is a curious lack, since it has nearly everything else. Instead, you must exit the program, answering "Are you sure" prompts, before you can even return to your application. Sidekick, by way of contrast, just disappears in a flash. It doesn't get in the way.

PC Tools will work as a normal program, or as a memory resident addition. The memory resident aspect of PC-Tools is both an asset and a liability. If everything works OK, then the ability to call up PC Tools and have it work from within an application is a real plus. It will even work with other memory-resident programs such as Sidekick. Some of the PC Tools utilities are very much oriented to this approach. The ability to format a disk from within an application, for example, is what makes this special format utility valuable. Otherwise, it would compete with the format utility provided with every copy of DOS.

The negatives of this approach are two. First, anything memory resident takes up memory. If your machine is not fully stocked with memory, or if you are running an application that is a memory hog, then you may suffer. A large spreadsheet, for example, will need available memory in order to run. If you have one or several memory resident programs, the size of the spreadsheet must be correspondingly smaller.

The second problem with memory residency is that it can be an iffy proposition. No one is quite sure what the program is doing in there. Are there conflicts? Perhaps you won't know until you lose a large and important file. While preparing this document, for example, we had both Sidekick and PC Tools in memory along with the word processor. Suddenly, the word processor commands began working erratically. At first, it looked like half the file was gone. We were required to exit the word processor and re-start the computer to clear the problem. Fortunately, no information was lost, but we still don't know what happened. And that's the second problem: it's risky.

Some of PC Tools' utilities are decidedly less risky than the originals provided by DOS. The FORMAT commands are a case in point. If you use the PC Tools variety, FORMAT won't hurt you, even if you format a disk that you didn't want to. It is a 'non-destructive' format that wipes out only the sign posts on the streets instead of the houses on the block. Through PC Tool's own utilities, you could recover from this very easily.

An option in PC Tool's MIRROR utility even allows you to keep track of all files you have deleted. Every time you perform such a command, MIRROR grabs the information on where the file once resided and saves it. For fragmented files with pieces scattered all over the disk, this would be particularly useful. Of course, if you re-write over the deleted sectors, then your data is lost anyway. But if you catch your mistake in time, this makes PC Tool's recovery task much easier.

| Norton Utility | Norton | PC Tools Skick | Mace |
|---|---|---|---|
| ASK | x | | |
| BEEP | x | | |
| Directory Sort | x | x | x |
| Disk Test | x | x | x |
| File Attributes | x | x | |
| File Find | x | x | |
| File Info | x | x | x |
| Format Recover | x | x | x |
| Safe Format | x | x | x |
| Directory Mirror | x | x | x |
| File Size | x | x | x |
| List Directories | x | x | |
| Prune & Graft | | x | |
| Line Print | x | x | |
| Norton CD | x | x | |
| Disk Map | x | x | x |
| Unerase | x | x | x |
| Edit at sector level | x | x | x |
| Quick UnErase | x | | x |
| Screen Attributes | x | | |
| Speed Disk | x | x | x |
| System Information | x | x | |
| Time Mark | x | | |
| Text Search | x | x | |

| | | | |
|---|---|---|---|
| UnRemove Directory | x | x | x |
| Volume Label | x | x | x |
| WipeDisk | x | | |
| WipeFile | x | | x |
| Copy files | | x | |
| Move files | | x | |
| Print files | | x | |
| Format a disk | | x | x |
| Park hard disk heads | | x | x |
| Backup System | | x | |
| Cache system | | x | x |
| Built in notepad | | x | x |
| ASCII table | | | x |
| Telecommunications | | | x |
| Calendar | | | x |
| Calculator | | | x |
| Memory Resident | | x | x |
| dBase fix program | | | x |
| Sqeeze directory | | | x |
| Vaccine | | | x |

## MACE UTILITIES

($150.00/$89.00: Paul Mace) The Mace Utilities are like Norton in that they provide utilities designed to help you recover from problems, plus speed up your disk. They are divided into three basic sections: Hot Rod, Recovery, and dB Fix. The Hot Rod utilities provide sorting and squeezing utilities designed to set up your hard disk for optimal performance. The Unfragment utility, for example, speeds up the disk by moving fragmented files into spaces which allow them to stay together. The Cache program allows you to set up memory for fast read and write activity.

The Recovery programs are strong on diagnosing and fixing hard disk errors. They allow unformatting and undeleting of disks and files; and they provide alternative format commands which can help prevent errors. The diagnostic utilities are much more strict than those found with DOS. Mace can search through your hard disk for suspect places and lock them out before damage occurs.

Like PC Tools, Mace sets up a secondary file on the disk which keeps track of all files comfortably away from the normal file allocation table. This is run at the beginning of a session with a small command in the AUTOEXEC.BAT. If this is present and your hard disk breaks, file recovery can be much easier.

Mace has a couple of unique features. A large part of the utilities is designed to recover damaged dBase files. In fact, there is a separate manual for this. Besides allowing recovery to take place, the utilities will teach you a lot about the internal architecture of dBase files. Considering the incredible market dominance of dBase, these utilities alone could be worth the price, about $45 at mail order prices.

Mace's Vaccine program in now unique among the utilities. Two levels of protection are involved. If you're worried about contamination of hard disks with those cute little tricks hackers like to pull, arming yourself with this anti-viral agent could be worthwhile. We recommend vaccine programs wherever terminals are available for general use.

The newest version, Mace 1990 (now sold by Fifth Generation Systems), has even more extensive vaccine programs, but as of this writing the new version has not yet shipped.

All the Mace utilities are tutorial in nature. Directions are clear and repeated often. If you actually read the documentation, you'll learn something and be a smarter PC user. If you are a "Quick Study," you'll learn a great deal. But Mace is not designed for the casual user, either. You needn't be a so-called Power User to use Mace effectively, but a Power User will be able to use Mace effectively, if that makes any sense.

## UTILITIES COMPARED

A strict comparison of available utilities may make Mace look at a disadvantage. But part of the beauty of Mace will never be told by a table such as we present. Norton can be compared to a Volvo. It is strictly utilitarian, but elegant in its approach. It is extremely competent. It is easy to use, almost to a fault. Everything works smoothly and quickly; and everything fits together extremely well. You don't really need a manual to know what is expected of you.

We've been around enough clones to say that IBM machines fit in the category. Taking a somewhat conservative approach, IBM hardware is good hardware. (So is, by the way, Hewlett Packard). IBM hardware is too expensive, and it will never test the outer envelope of power and technology, but it works. So does Norton.

Mace is like a 300ZX with a radar detector—more fun. It's not as slick as Norton. Instead, it assumes you are an intelligent person, can read, and can follow directions. Mace has an "attitude" about it that is reflected in the way the programs run, and even in the manual. Instead of proclaiming "This Page Intentionally Blank" Mace proclaims, "This page blank as a salesman's memory," or "This page intentionally empty like a politician's promise." Throughout the documentation Paul Mace TALKS to you. He admonishes you to pay attention. He tells you how hardware manufacturers have cut corners at your expense. He explains just why his programs work and how you can help make them work by not messing up.

Mace can work through fancy menus, just like everyone else; but we get the impression they are there because of competitive pressures. His utilities are all worthwhile; there isn't a fluff program among them. In that sense, it may look like he doesn't provide as much as something like PC Tools. Not true.

From a support standpoint, Mace is dedicated to recovering your data. He knows the phones are always busy; and he has a unique approach. If they are, he says to send a telegram, and he'll call you. He promises to investigate every complaint (and hopes there are none.) He tells you to relax, take a deep breath, and read the manual first. Mace is fun and geared toward results, yet many of the features are designed to prevent you from hurting yourself. Mace won't hurt you either. If Mace is about to do something that will alter your data, he'll tell you ahead of time and admonish you, once again, to read the directions.

PC Tools is attempting to be everything to everybody. But like many programs, it suffers somewhat from creeping featuritis. We like a great many of its features, but it's just a little cumbersome to use, compared to the other two major programs reviewed here. Certainly from a features standpoint it wins by a mile. It has more of everything, in a good mix, than any of the others. In theory, PC Tools is all you need. But we have this nagging feeling that there's too much there; and that it will be to our detriment. Our problems with conflicts when memory resident have made us a little gun shy of the program. We managed to recover without data loss the first time, but recovery from data loss is what PC Tools is supposed to protect you from, not cause by using. What, then, will it do to us next time? Yet PC Tools inclusion of a complete backup utility, in our view, is worth the price of the program all by itself.

Comparing strictly from features, PC Tools and Sidekick pack the best value for the dollar. Between the two, you have everything. Sidekick makes up for the poor notepad in PC Tools, plus it adds a calculator and ASCII table which we find valuable. PC Tools itself provides every utility of any of the other packages. When you add up features mathematically, PC Tools wins.

We feel Norton is still necessary. The ASK command is central to our batch processing system in the last chapter. Its sector editing is superb as well, better than PC Tools, and, in our opinion, more elegantly implemented than Mace. Yet Mace has the best of Norton and the best of PC Tools all wrapped into one. We like it as well; it is an education.

All three utilities now provide a utility that will help you recover from a hard disk crash. PC Tools calls this "MIRROR" and Mace calls it "RXBAK." Norton calls it "Format Recover." They all do approximately the same thing. They keep an extra copy of the FAT table and directory entries comfortably away from the two adjacent copies at the beginning of a hard disk. If that part of the disk gets trashed, you're safe. When the disk crashes, you may be able to recover.

**We strongly suggest you install one of these programs on every hard disk.**

In the final analysis, we suggest you get all three programs: Norton Advanced, Mace, and PC Tools, and also Sidekick, though that one is in a slightly different category. (We're not convinced Sidekick Plus, the newest and more expensive upgrade, is necessary.) Study them all, then pick the best features of each. Remember that you are attempting to create an applications toolbox for yourself, in order to support your users. Carpenters have more than one hammer, so there's no reason why you can't have more than one utility, even if they do overlap.

## SPINRITE II

($89.00: Gibson Management) Spinrite is currently available only from Steve Gibson himself, not through mail order houses. The program's main purpose in life is to re-format your hard disk without destroying data that is already on it. Gibson's claim is that hard disks gradually lose their magnetism at a low level. The normal everyday reading and writing of a hard disk does not touch this low level; therefore, it is never refreshed by another zap from the disk drive heads. This program lifts off the information from a hard disk a section at a time. It then reformats the disk in that section, and then places the data back on top of the new formatting. Gibson makes the claim that if you use this program on a hard disk a couple of times a year, you will *never* have any problems with it.

For a mere $89.00, we're willing to believe this enough to use it in conjunction with proper backup procedures, but we can't help but notice Gibson's disclaimers in the front matter of his documentation. Anyone who has been through a disk crash, large or small, will do anything to avoid it. If it turns out Gibson's bravado is just that, fine. At least we tried.

The other major operation Spinrite performs is to change the "interleave factor" on a hard disk. The interleave factor comes into play as the disk spins around at 3600 RPM. Because the disk is spinning so quickly, the read head of many disks, particularly cheaper ones, can't keep its act together fast enough to read disk sectors which are side by side. It must wait for another revolution before it is ready to read (or write) again. To circumvent this problem, engineers build in an interleave factor that sets up the disk to be read differently. The "next" sector of a disk is not right next door, but several doors away from the original sector. Therefore, the read heads have time to recoup their losses before the "next" sector comes around to be read. The setting of this interleave factor is under software control. An interleave factor of three or four is the most common we have seen, but Gibson says most hard disks are set incorrectly. Spinrite changes the interleave factor for optimal performance. He's so sure that your hard disk speed will increase that he offers you money back if it does not.

The heart of Spinrite performs both these major operations at once. It checks for bad sectors as well, putting the drive through a torture test designed to ferret out sectors that aren't bad yet, but will be. The most brutal level of this "scrubbing" took a mere eleven and a half hours on our 30MB Seagate hard disk. It's the kind of thing you turn on, turn off the monitor, and hope that by the next morning it is done. One would trust that eleven hours is enough time to accomplish a very thorough job.

There are disappointments to the package. First of all, it won't work on quite a few hard disks. Plus Development Corporation's hard cards are a case in point. These are extremely reliable hard cards that garner a price premium, but Spinrite won't touch them. It also won't touch some cards controlled by early Western Digital or Adaptec controllers. It doesn't like some RLL encoding techniques; and it won't work on Priam hard drives.

Copy protection can be a problem with programs such as this, and it was with the first version. The newest, Spinrite 2, is capable of patching around protection schemes that demand proper physical placement on a disk.

Actually, no major software vendor continues to use copy protection, at least on MS-DOS machines. Even Lotus has dropped protection. Hopefully, this won't be a problem, unless you use a lot of game or education software, much of which is still protected.

Gibson's software isn't protected, of course. However, he does have licensing requirements which are not apparent on the advertising. You originally purchase Spinrite for personal use only. You can use it on any hard disks which you personally own. But corporations are supposed to license Spinrite separately for every hard disk, to the tune of $25.00 for every extra disk they use. Consultants can use Spinrite on client's disks for $10.00 a shot; and value added resellers can use it free, as long as they include Gibson's sales literature with the products they sell.

Gibson also includes a sophisticated head parking utility with the package. We recommend the entire package for use anywhere hard disks are.

## ATSIFT

Many of the utilities discussed in this chapter concern manipulation of entire files. All the hard disk utilities, for example, work on the assumption that you wish to move, backup, restore, and otherwise keep whole files on the disk. With some of the utilities you can edit individual bytes in a file, but so far we don't have a utility that can truly manipulate files themselves, on a wholesale basis.

ATSIFT is a small utility program which does just that. It allows you to manipulate the contents of a file, in a limited way. Originally published by Vertex Systems in Los Angeles, repeated attempts to contact the firm have failed. They are no longer in the phone directory, Information does not have their listing, and letters to the firm have been returned with no forwarding address.

If we read the copyright law correctly, this means this little program may be fair game. Repeated calls in an attempt to find the business which originally sold it to us have been to no avail.

The program is actually a small part of a package designed to transfer files from the older Apple II microcomputers to MS-DOS computers. The system consisted of utility programs that would copy either Apple DOS 3.3 or Apple CP/M files to the IBM via an "Apple Turnover" card which plugged into the IBM. The special Turnover card was necessary because of the strange way the Apple II disks held their data. The genius behind this was Steve Wozniak, co-founder of Apple Computer along with Steve Jobs. Known as The Woz, Steve is widely considered an electronic genius. His method of disk encoding has itself been incorporated into an integrated chip called the IWM, the Integrated Woz Machine.

Those who know the technical details of such things say the method is utter genius. But it meant that copying files from an Apple disk to any other disk presents problems. The Turnover plugged into a slot of an IBM and allowed the transfer to take place. Utility programs handled most of the details.

ATSIFT is one of those utility programs. It will change Wordstar files to ASCII files, strip the high bit from files, add the line feed character after a known carriage return, or remove a carriage return after a line feed. It will also strip a plain carriage return, or remove a carriage return/line feed combination. In addition, it will replace any "string" with another.

A carriage return is designated in hexadecimal jargon as 0D (13 decimal, "Control-M" or just "CR"). A line feed is designated as 0A hexadecimal (10 decimal, "Control-J" or just "LF"). These physical characters are encoded in text files, normally (you guessed it) at the ends of lines. The utility is designed to work with various word processors, some of which place carriage returns at the ends of lines, some of which don't.

When you are attempting to translate one word processor file into another, this sort of utility can be very handy. The lack of one or the other of these characters can make the text scroll far to the right of the screen boundaries, or be compressed all into one line at the top, or both at once. Conversely, too many of these characters can force double or triple spacing when you don't want it. "ASCII" means the characters are encoded the same way, but it doesn't mean they are strung together the same way. It can be confusing.

Many word processors have such utilities, but they are rarely as all-encompassing. All word processors have the ability to "import" Wordstar files just as all data base systems can import dBase files. But they don't always offer the raw processing power offered by this one utility.

Because Vertex Systems is now apparently out of business, we will include a copy of this program on the free disk offer detailed in the appendix. If we do find the copyright owner of this program, we may need to rescind this part of the offer. We're still checking.

## CHECK-IT

So far we have been discussing utilities that can manipulate files or play with a hard disk. Those are all important, of course, and they may comprise one of your major activities. However, there is the hardware to consider. Unfortunately, there are problems with hardware, memory, and peripheral devices that no hard disk utility can help you with.

Fortunately, several utilities have recently come on the market designed to help diagnose hardware problems and memory problems. They certainly don't do everything you would like, but they are a step in the right direction.

Check-it is one such piece of diagnostic software, from Touchstone Systems, which seeks to diagnose and report on system problems and performance. It will run on any PC system, whatever the vintage, as long as it's MS-DOS based. Its basic operations are to decipher the configuration of the target system, diagnose the components for reliability, and to measure system performance.

## CONFIGURATION

The configuration portion of the system tells you what you have in the system. This includes the date and manufacturer of your BIOS chips. This all-important information may be crucial, for example, if you are attempting to install a hard disk on a true-blue IBM with a BIOS date before 10/27/82. The answer: You can't.

The program reports the type of processor, the DOS version, presence of several types of memory, ports, and disk drives. It also tells you interrupt assignments, once again, crucial information should you be attempting to attach two devices to the same interrupt.

For example, we installed a desktop publishing system last year that included a Microsoft Mouse and a large Taxan Crystalview monitor. There was also a scanner on the system. Things worked fine for a few months until the monitor's CGA portion began to go bad. Everything worked well in high-resolution mode, necessary for using Ventura and the graphics software, but once you "dropped to DOS" you couldn't even see the screen.

So, reluctantly, we packed the entire thing up and shipped it back to Taxan, along with the special video card that drives this particular monitor. A few weeks went by and the monitor was returned. We tore apart the machine, reinstalled everything, and tried to make it work.

No dice. This time the high-resolution portion of the monitor was bad. We tested out the system by taking it to another computer and trying it there. Same symptoms exactly. Therefore, it couldn't be the computer, right?

Numerous phone calls determined it was not the monitor that was probably bad, but the card itself. Several weeks later we finally got a call from Taxan saying the card was fine, so what was our problem? We insisted. But eventually the card was returned "No Trouble Found." Taxan said it worked fine.

Well, nothing to do but to re-install and try again, perhaps a little more carefully. Upon looking at the jumpers on the video card we discovered they had been changed from where we had set them earlier. We looked up the jumpers in the very cryptic documentation. It seems the "interrupt" chosen was different. We looked into the matter and discovered there was a conflict with the Microsoft Mouse, which was using the same interrupt exactly. We hadn't found this out when we installed on a different computer, because that one, too, had a Microsoft Mouse, using the same interrupt controller.

Surprise. Once we switched the interrupt, everything worked beautifully. That's what Check-it will help you do. Had we had this information then, the problem would have been patently obvious. Instead, we wasted a few weeks figuring it all out.

Programs of this nature will often claim you need no longer take apart your computer to find out what's in it. Though this is a noble goal, the fact you have this information at your fingertips may not be quite as labor-saving as advertisements would have you imagine. You'll still have to take the cover off. The combination of information, however, will give you a very good idea of what is happening inside your system.

## DIAGNOSTICS

Check-it tests memory in several different ways, tests all the drives, the system board itself, ports, the printer, extensive video tests, a keyboard test, and even a mouse test. Loopback plugs for the port tests are optional. The keyboard test is typical and not much different than others we have seen, graphics being the only difference.

One unique portion of Check-it's operation is the inclusion of memory board testing which will high-light a suspect chip with a graphics display. Anyone who has ever had to decipher some cryptic self-test message ("2001 error"—now that's helpful!) on memory will immediately see the usefulness of this feature.

To achieve this usefulness, unfortunately, takes a little extra work. You must first inform Check-it what type of memory board you have installed and how the chips are laid out on the board. Touchstone admits this is the most difficult part of the configuration process. An extensive READ ME file attempts to help the unwary through this decoding. But once it's done, it's dynamite to use.

## PERFORMANCE TESTING

Check-it has several tests for system performance which are similar to Norton's SysInfo test in that they attempt to compare speeds across systems. Norton's test has been widely criticized as a narrow measure of performance. Not only that, PC makers have also been suspected of "writing to" the Norton test by implementing a "Norton Detector" circuit which tests for the Norton test, then provides an artificially high performance benchmark. As far as we know, no one has confirmed the widespread use of this technique, but it does crop up in the computer press now and again.

Check-it uses the Dhrystone test to determine CPU speed, and also has test for video speed, math speed, and several tests of the hard disk.

## AN ASIDE ON SPEED

Video testing brings up an interesting point. The fastest CPU in the known universe can be severely bogged down by a couple of factors. One is the type of video card you have installed in your system.

We have a friend who just purchased a 386/20MHz machine from PC Brand, one of the larger mail order firms. He is using his old video board, an 8-bit design which is half CGA and half high-resolution for desktop publishing.

The CPU speed of his new system is very fast, 21.0 on the Norton scale, but his use of the 8-bit video board shows for any video-intensive operation, especially graphics. There is *not* a comparable performance increase on the video-portion of his computer. It does move faster, it is true, but not the three times faster his new computer moves compared to the old one.

The second potential drag on a fast CPU is the hard disk itself. Placing a 60ms hard disk in a 386 machine is like pulling a wagon full of bricks with a racing bike. The potential of the bike will never be realized. This is why ESDI and SCSI hard drives with access in the 16ms range are frequently advertised with the higher systems. They offer much faster access and much faster transfer of data from the disk into your computer.

## OPERATION

Check-it's operation is hassle-free. It's easy to use, with drop-down windows along the top of the screen and intuitive operation. The system will log the entire testing process to a disk file or printer. You can even batch the whole thing and make it run on automatic pilot.

We did have a few minor problems with its use. It couldn't find the clock/calendar, though the documentation warns this might happen. And the system listed our 1.44MB three inch floppy as a 1.2MB drive. We have some DIP switch settings wrong. We know that, but the software did not detect that something was wrong.

There is no copy protection on Check-it. They do have a "guilt screen" ala Lotus and dBase, but we ought to be able to handle those. Documentation is informative and complete. We like this software and are happy to have it. Cost is $149.00. Check-It 2.1: Touchstone Software, 909 Electric Ave., Seal Beach, FL 90740. 800-531-0450.

## SYSTEM SLEUTH

We received version 2 of System Sleuth about the same time as Check-it. This software does not purport to be diagnostic in the same way as Check-it, so it's not quite fair to include them as selling an equivalent product. It performs the same sort of configuration analysis as Check-it, but does more of it.

In other words, it will report on nearly everything Check-it does, and adds several important features. One is a TSR program map, for example, that can tell you just what is loaded in your system that may be affecting performance. Did you know the DOS MODE command is actually a memory resident program? So is COMMAND.COM and any number of little programs running in your AUTOEXEC.BAT besides your friend Sidekick, lots of memory buffers, and space for extra files.

Add those all up and load a memory hog program like dBase IV or Ventura publisher, and guess what happens. A warm boot won't even work. You get to cut the power and start over. Of course, since you have all this stuff in AUTOEXEC, you'll have to terminate the batch as it starts and muck around in there until you can remove some of those files.

From that standpoint alone, Systems Sleuth is an eye-opener. It also tries valiantly to save you from opening the case, far more than other programs in this category. One of its operations is to read all the ROMs on the cards stuck in slots in the back of your PC. It reads each address space and attempts to decipher what is there. It doesn't always succeed, but it gives you instant evidence of conflicts if you are trying to double up on memory space.

The memory information available via System Sleuth is very extensive. The program allows you to view memory in situ, and provides easy ways for doing so.

### OPERATION

Operation of System Sleuth is straight-forward. There is quite a lot of information presented, and it is sometimes cryptic. All of it won't be of use to even the more sophisticated user.

There were a couple of interesting anomalies to the program. It reports we have a whopping amount of extended memory; we have none. And it seems to have trouble figuring out the expanded memory we do have. In other respects it agrees with Check-it, so if the programs are reporting erroneously, they both are.

System Sleuth 2.0, DTG, Inc., 7439 La Palma Ave., Suite 278, Buena Park, CA 92620. 714-994-7400. $100.00.

### SUMMARY

The utilities above will help the PC Guru manage PCs more easily. They probably are not in the same mix the Guru will use for his or her own machine. Nor are they the same mix of utilities that would be used by the typical user on a daily basis. The intent is to provide a toolbox of useful utilities that can support the management of PCs.

Unfortunately, they are not all you need. Local hardware and software will govern some of the utilities that are necessary. This is particularly true of utilities that govern expansion cards from various manufacturers. These are usually developed by the individual manufacturer to take advantage of quirks of their own machinery. Ironically, some of them won't work unless the card itself works. So if the card is broken, you can't run the utilities to diagnose it. (This is true of the PC Breakthru speed-up cards, for example.)

# APPLICATIONS TOOLBOX (USER VERSION)

Microcomputers have freed the masses. This isn't intended as a political statement, particularly; it's a fact. Before micros, employees of any organization of any size were forced to use computing power in the way the organization dictated, period. In fact, many users were not allowed close to any computer at all. Perhaps a terminal was allowed on the desk, but the terminal had no processing power for itself, and users were forced to use programs supplied by the organization.

As a result, all users of word processing in an organization used the word processor associated with the big system, or none at all. They used the accounting system available on the big system, or none at all. This wasn't always done in a sinister way, if it ever was. That was all that was available.

Once micros showed up, users suddenly had more applications available to them than ever before. Not only that, the applications were well done! Word processing on a micro meant you had more features available. Does anyone seriously contend that a mainframe or mini-based word processor holds a candle to WordPerfect? Sure, the guys in the computer room were sneering at the micros. After all, what COBOL compiler could one of those run, ha ha! And you call that an operating system? It doesn't do anything!

Had these same folks dBase III on their mainframe, they would have been ecstatic. Of course, you'd have to call it something else, like VSAM/OX2 Version 8.4, the latest in data management. Still, that dot prompt would have been like honey to a bear. Instead, the users got the good stuff while the big computer folks were allowed to mess around with the typical, esoteric, buggy software packages that cost $100,000 for mainframes and still purport to be developed programs.

Micros often infiltrate an organization from the bottom up, brought in by employees who realize what productive tools they are and buy one for themselves out of desperation. The cost of a micro plus software is often far far less than monthly maintenance on a big mainframe, yet the software is often better. Eventually the corporation comes around and figures out they have micros sitting on desks. Where did they come from, and out of who's budget?

They also have different software everywhere, probably different hardware, and no sense of order whatsoever. Meanwhile the computer aficionados are proclaiming their software to be the best ever.

"My WordPerfect is better than your Wordstar!" they say, to which comes a reply from a third party.

"Everyone knows that serious writers use XyWrite III. You're stuff is pure junk, and slow besides."

And, of course, the Apple guys are talking about throwing files in proprietary garbage cans with mice and how they are going to change the world. There are even a few people who proclaim the Commodore 64 to be perfectly appropriate for business. They have as much clout, surely, as the CP/M diehards who claim 8-bit computers can still do an adequate job with their 8 inch floppy discs.

Of course, every one of these people can prove to you how their favorite program has increased their productivity exponentially. No doubt, they are correct. But they're like the homeowner who finally succumbed to buying a microwave oven. Now able to enjoy the advantages of nuking a potato in seven minutes, the person erroneously attributes the increase in efficiency to Sears or GE, not to microwave ovens in general.

You can imagine the attitude of the corporate brass as their automation experts, the folks running the minis and mainframes, are filling them full of these horror stories. Suddenly there are all sorts of different machines with different disk formats which can't be read across the board. It's not just that Apples can't talk to IBM, but IBM PCs can't talk to IBM AT class machines, either. Those disk drives might look the same, but a 1.2MB drive on an AT will not write reliably onto a disk that fits into a 360K drive on a PC. That means you can swap disks from a PC to an AT, but you can't swap disks from an AT to a PC, at least with any reliability! Now throw in the new 3.5" disk drive popularized by Apple's Macintosh and IBM's new PS/2 line, and you begin to see the problem. And we haven't even gotten to software incompatibilities yet.

Not wanting their own mini Tower of Babble, it is no wonder that many organizations set out to standardize on machines and hardware. Not surprisingly, most corporations at least initially settled on IBM, MS-DOS type machines over Apples. They might have chosen Apple had they realized micros were real before IBM, as they say, "legitimized" the market.

Software standardization came next, with the majority of corporations choosing Lotus 1-2-3 over Supercalc, dBase over R:Base and others, and WordPerfect over anything else. When the corporation is paying for all this, it's much easier to enforce approved lists for hardware and software. With smaller organizations faced with individual software purchased with individual funds, the problem is more difficult.

## IMPORTANCE OF STANDARDS

In individualistic America, it's taken as a matter of faith that we can all do our own thing, that we can develop our own methods, and use our own software. From a personal standpoint, it is an affront for someone else to tell us what we should use in the way of software and hardware. This has not been lost on the makers of "alternative" products. Apple's "1984" commercials, for example, portrayed the IBM world as a bunch of lemmings marching off a cliff, to be liberated to freedom if only they would turn to Apples. Another showed Apple liberating the masses from Big Brother.

As Apple turned "pro" and essentially kicked out the original guiding lights of the company, this sentiment lessened, at least overtly, and Apple no longer takes such a direct approach. Instead, they use the "Man buys Apple, keeps job" approach, spearheaded with the Macintosh and desktop publishing.

Apple's complaint of persecution by corporations is certainly justified. But many Apple aficionados take this to an extreme. Like the pilgrims on the Mayflower, once they get Apples, they do their best to persecute any other religion.

But the idea that the individual with the individual micro single-handedly changed the world persists. This is particularly true when individual employees have bucked the glacial tide of institutional change to learn, use, and prove that microcomputers are a necessary part of productivity. Why, then, should they change to so-called "standards"?

If you encounter this, enforcing standards may be difficult, if not impossible. When the only good application ever done in the entire organization has been done with Revelation instead of dBase, maybe that will be enough to sway opinion to making that a standard instead of one of the more inferior systems available.

OK, then make that the standard. Hopefully, someone else in the State also uses the same program, the software producer will be in business five years from now, and it has been used by enough people to ensure there are no fatal bugs in there waiting to zap your data. Hopefully.

But standards themselves are necessary. Otherwise, everyone will be using a different word processor, a different spreadsheet, and a different data base system. Then, when you want to share files, work on a budget together, or produce a document in pieces that can be melded into a whole, guess who gets stuck with the work of putting the pieces of this eggshell back together again?

You do.

You get to put out the fires. You get to patiently explain that you can't load WordPerfect files directly into Microsoft Word because the internal file formats are different. Unless one or the other has provided a direct translation utility, you must convert the file to straight-ASCII, then load it into the other word processor, where all the formatting needs to be re-done. You might be able to use IBM's DCA (Document Control Architecture) as long as DCA supports the features of both word processors in question, as well as DCA itself. And that's an easy one. Now let's do data base systems and spreadsheets between different types of computer systems.

Yes, it's possible to do. Maybe some of the software utilities mentioned above will help you. Great! But it's still a lot of work; and that's not proving the productivity we're all ostensibly after. It's the same argument for the MARC format and authority files in libraries. No one ever accused MARC of being the most user-friendly data format available, but most librarians will grudgingly admit that a standard nation-wide format is proving useful over the long term. Somebody may have to lose. And that means someone, even you, may need to put away that esoteric, neat little program no one else knows exists in favor of a better supported, more universal alternative.

Standards are also important for your own sanity. In the final analysis, you can't possibly learn a multitude of programs to the depth necessary to really support it. If your organization is big enough to allow this, then perhaps there is a cadre of gurus, all with their own specialties, ready to run out at every fire call. We're assuming, however, that you have limited time and personnel resources available. If someone else increases their productivity at the expense of yours, what has the organization gained? With some semblance of standards you will be able to concentrate on learning a few programs in depth to the "support level." Your argument, then, will be that you only support dBase and R:Base, so if someone insists on getting another program, leave you out of it.

The arguments for one program over another often boil down to emotional preference, particularly among beginners. But after you have learned four or five word processors to a depth necessary to write long documents and learn all its features, you become rather cynical about learning another one. If you stick with major packages which are close in features anyway, switching will provide only marginal benefits. If someone is suggesting a switch that offers only a few benefits, then perhaps it ought to be resisted. In today's climate, the competitors usually implement each other's new and improved features in a few months anyway.

Standards might also bring some surprising benefits. We are continually amazed at how much even a neophyte user can coax out of supposedly difficult programs. Ventura Publisher, for example, has this "reputation" of being cryptic. We helped a new computer user install Ventura not long ago. It was a complicated procedure full of pitfalls. Eventually, the thing worked. We left this poor guy in the middle of the tutorial and told him to call us when he got into trouble. The best thing to do then is to take the phone off the hook.

But two days later he came into the office with the slickest looking brochure you have ever seen. His shadow boxes were particularly impressive.

"How did you do that?" we asked incredulously. We had never been able to accomplish the same task.

"Yeah, well. This isn't really a box, it's an oval. And the front to back operation won't work on a box, so you can't get the shadow. But it will work on the oval. So I just lengthened the oval until it looked like a box. You can see the slightly rounded corners. It's all in its own frame, otherwise it will repeat throughout every page. Then you just flip it, and there you are!"

There you are, indeed! We'd given up on the operation and never would have known. But the fact someone else close by was using the same software for the same sorts of operations provided an entirely new dimension to learning the product for all of us. If he'd been using Pagemaker, we wouldn't have paid much attention.

The real point here is that standards are not sinister. They aren't intended to stifle innovation, prevent creativity, and make people conform for the sake of conformity. The above example rather well proves the opposite. Software standards are like a standard for languages. The official language in this country is English. It's nice to know other languages; and perhaps Spanish out to be a required second alternative. And other foreign languages are necessary in certain circumstances. We all suffer because we don't do better in this realm. But if we all spoke different languages *to the exclusion of the standard,* there would be no communication.

## THE PROBLEM OF REVIEWS

If you are not yet screaming "Fascist" at us for suggesting standards may be appropriate (You do drive on the right hand side of the road, don't you?), come with us into the realm of the software review. They're sort of like book reviews, really. Many of them are short and sweet, an announcement and thumbnail sketch. Reviews in sources like *InfoWorld* are a little more detailed. Here there is some notion that reviews ought to test and report in a certain defined manner by addressing specific issues as ease of use, support, error-handling, and so forth. They even present a resulting score on a scale of one to ten, frequently rating separate packages of the same class side-by-side.

The scores become a handle on which the disgruntled manufacturer places the argument, "How come you rated us a six and the other guy a seven on this feature when his can't even do belly-flops?"

*PC Week,* the major competitor to *InfoWorld,* takes a different approach. Seeking to be better by being physically larger (a time-honored technique) they review software by listing every possible feature each package has. The listings are as comprehensive as you could possibly imagine. The tables and charts run to pages. Certainly if you're worried that the latest revision of *Redundo*

*Word Version 5.12* might not have double underlining in italics with word-wrap, this is the place to check.

A step up from *InfoWorld* reviews are those provided by the comprehensive testing services such as *Software Digest*. It's not that *InfoWorld*'s reviews are not as good, it's that *Software Digest*'s Reviews are so comprehensive. *InfoWorld* reviews walk through a new house with the critical eye of a potential new owner, noting dust in the corner and, perhaps, misplaced light switches. *Software Digest* hires a registered structural engineer, crawls through the attic and under the crawl space, and takes a comprehensive inventory of all spiders, mice, and cockroaches. They have all of *InfoWorld*, all of *PC Week*, and garner opinions from an entire herd of users, rather than just one reviewer opening up the package for the first time, shackled by the weight of his or her own opinions.

For those who truly want to study the subject with a view toward definitive answers, we suggest you obtain subscriptions to the above three publications, plus *PC Magazine, PC World, Byte,* and *The National Review*. Study everything in those places for at least a year. Then you'll know which software product to buy.

The problem, then, as stated in the paragraph above, is an embarrassment of riches. There's too much out there. Many of the products which are available are from small publishers who may or may not be around in a year or two. For a book publisher, that's OK. That fits in with how we buy books anyway. We can't buy them all, so we wait for a one paragraph review in *LJ* or *Booklist* or *Kirkus,* then buy the book, in multiple copies, if need be. Since one book is likely to result in a miniscule percentage of the book budget (our books take about .00004% each) one bad purchase is no big deal. Besides, you don't have to read it. The patron has to read it, but only if he or she wants to.

Software, however, tends to be expensive. Surely, prices are coming down for many types of software that appeal to the masses. But vertical market software is still absurdly expensive; and prices are unlikely to decline much further. Why? One reason is because the production of software is labor intensive. That's all software is, really, a set of laborious instructions for a computer that somebody thought up and wrote down. The machines will come down in price, but the software will tend upwards.

Secondly, as software has become more sophisticated, the number of years of labor needed to produce one comprehensive software project is astounding. Dozens, if not hundreds of programmers work on projects such as dBase IV. The price of the physical disks is nothing. But added to this substantial development time are distribution and advertising costs that can also be large.

As a user, you are faced with the prospect of purchasing relatively more expensive software products from this ever-growing array of offerings. Let us guess what your software budget may be. It probably is nowhere near the cost of the machine on which you wish to run the software (even though it ought to be). It probably will come out of the book budget over the Acquisition Librarian's dead body.

"What? You want to buy a $695 copy of dBase IV for EACH microcomputer, and you want to take it out of *my* budget? Expletive deleted!"

Perhaps you can squeeze the Supplies budget a little; or maybe Capital Equipment if no one looks too closely. But even if you do manage to have a lot of money for software, you can't afford to make too many mistakes. This may make you take a more conservative approach than you otherwise might.

Another problem with software is that, unlike hardware, it is a subjective subject. Hardware can be evaluated using benchmark programs and other devices. It either will or will not perform to a given level. Norton's SI index will show how fast it works, at least according to SI. It will or will not run standard MS-DOS software; it does or does not have 3.5" drives. Certainly there are subjective considerations: do you like amber colored monitors or green? But the point is that hardware will or won't pass a given test. There is little argument.

Software is subjective. Who says using a Mouse with Microsoft Word is easier than function keys with WordPerfect? Who says a dot prompt is worse than the letter "R" on the screen, or that instructions appearing at the top of the screen are inherently better than those which appear at the bottom?

**With software, the better program is the one you know how to use; the worst one is the one you know nothing about.**

This is not just a problem with users grown fond of their personal choice. It is also a problem with reviewers and, sadly, salespeople in retail stores. They recommend what they know. Often, they don't know a lot. You get the benefit of this knowledge or lack thereof, whether you know it or not.

We've been through this a number of times. We once purchased The Data Factory for an Apple II to hold a mere mailing list. That was in the days before dBase and much of anything else. We were assured this was absolutely the slickest piece of software since the Woz figured out the memory refresh cycles on an Apple.

We bought the package and quickly reached its limitations. It was written in BASIC and copy protected. But through one of the various bugs we managed to crash into the system, accidentally, but fortunately in a reproducible manner. Listing the program we found innumerable bugs staring at us. A call to the company found them more upset that we had listed their program than about a missing RETURN from a GOSUB we were reporting. "But that's not allowed!" they said. Missing RETURNS are not allowed, we agreed. We struggled with this program for over a year.

Ultimately, we were forced to write our own recovery programs to get the data back out of the Data Factory and into something more palatable, in this case the silky smooth (then) dBase II. dBase had just come on the market and was advertised as an alternative to bilge pumps, which all suck. Since then we've read many shocked reviews about the poor taste of that original ad, but no truer words were ever spoken. Watch out. This could happen to you.

The discussion below will detail the current state of the software industry in the categories we've established. *Our recommendations are neither mandatory nor exhaustive.* They are quite intentionally conservative and presuppose a certain mind set. That mind set consists of the following caveats:

1. You don't want to make a mistake on a software product that may be of limited usefulness or be from a publisher that has already filed for Chapter 11. We've been a party to this syndrome in the past. Suddenly, that program advertised to do all things for all people is no longer supported. We once bought Perfect Writer for an old CP/M machine after believing the ads; and it NEVER WORKED! That programmer left and is no longer available to consult. The company folded. There will be no more updates. Anything can happen. This is happening today. Software programs are advertised that aren't available. They call this "vapor ware." Our discussion below is as much based on market forces as it is on the strengths of the individual packages involved.

2. You are attempting to pull together an "Applications Toolbox" of general-purpose programs that can be used in a variety of ways. In other words, the discussion below is not attempting to explicitly define the best newspaper indexing program available in America today (There aren't any: trust me). An "Applications Toolbox" gets you started with a skill-saw, a hammer, and a drill. If you want a radial arm saw and a mitre box, feel free.

3. You want the best programs available without spending an inordinate amount of money. Sometimes the very best pro-

grams in a given category are great, but they just happen to cost a thousand dollars apiece. Or their policies mean that you must pay extra money for "runtime licenses" and other paraphernalia in order for the product to be truly useful. Or, horror, they may be copy protected.

4. Training is probably an issue for you. The packages below, generally speaking, are packages typically taught by training institutes, whether they be private or community classes. You do not want to find yourself in a position of deciding outside training resources are needed only to find the package you selected for general distribution is not taught by the firms in this business. In fact, research into packages should include a brochure from the local software training firms to see what is available. This may help you make a decision.

5. We do not want to hedge our bets by giving you some watered down recommendations to try anything, because after all, this is a free country and all. Too many times those who are in a position to recommend simply won't do it. They say to choose something to fit your needs when you are asking what those needs might be. They say there is a vast world of choices out there when you know that already and are trying to narrow them down. In other words, were we to pretend objectivity and fairness to avoid criticism, we could make no recommendations. Safe for us, bad for you.

   We realize these recommendations are conservative. Surely those who fit in the categories we've discussed above will cry foul in an attempt to push their very favorite, super duper program as the real answer. But recommending some little-known or alternative software package does not guarantee innovation, particularly without that the protagonists continual presence to explain the little features that make it so special. In fact, our *recommendations are not always our personal favorites*. We are often torn between what may be the best, and the inertia of our own training which makes us reluctant to give up a tool memorized for marginal benefit elsewhere.

6. Many of the prime movers in software are very expensive. You're supposed to buy one copy for every machine. That's what the law says. Therefore, if there is a robust alternative available which mimics the original, we list it as well.

## Data Base Management Systems (DBMS)

Data Base Management Systems are one of the three or four most common types of software available for micros. There is no mystery to their inherent function. They contain files of data, hooked together in mysterious and arcane ways. In theory, you can get the reports you want on the information in those files in ways that make sense to your organization. In practice, data base systems are a great way to lose your data.

dBase (in its current incarnation as dBase IV) is the market leader. Other major players include R:Base by Microrim, Reflex, by Borland, Paradox, by Borland, Revelation, by Cosmos, Q&A (very highly rated), PFS Professional File, Eureka, and VP Info. There are dozens more, and new ones surely to follow. And it does not follow that the market leaders are the best. Sometimes the one lurking in the basement of the marketplace may be the best system ever to be invented, stifled only by lack of marketing skill and clout. We recognize that the entrenched base of software and hardware may not be the best available, even from objective standards.

Surely R:Base, by Microrim is a case in point. In test after test, R:Base beats dBase III + every time. *Software Digest* shows R:Base to be best. So do *PC Magazine, InfoWorld,* and others. R:Base is rated easier to use, more powerful, more versatile, in nearly every category. Yet it is dBase that enjoys an entrenched market share that has made Ashton Tate one of the largest software corporations in the world. R:Base has enjoyed some success, some converts, and it isn't going to go away any time soon. Nor is it about to unseat dBase as the data base of choice for most users.

One of the reasons for this is the hefty after-market that has developed for dBase applications. Not just a data base system, dBase is a programming language. Developers have taken to the language with gusto, to a certain extent shutting Ashton-Tate out of the process. Compilers have been developed for dBase which allow the programming code to be run without the necessity of purchasing dBase itself. Clones have been brought to the market which are compatible with dBase, yet do not share the actual machine code. DBXL, by Wordtech Systems, for example, has managed to garner a respectable market share all by itself just by pretending to work like dBase, but at a significantly lower price.

In fact, dBase has been so successful that it is has lost control of the dBase language itself. Third parties have made many enhancements to make up for features lacking in dBase, and they are considering forming a language standard just as has been done with COBOL, Fortran, and other languages since. You can't easily copyright a language, particularly after it gets popular. Ashton-Tate still maintains they have rights to the language itself, but industry observers doubt this can be enforced.

Due to this success, other software publishers have included features which allow their programs to read and even write to the dBase file structure. R:Base must do it to survive, and so do many other software products, few of them actually competitive data base management system products. Instead, they may be spreadsheet or graphics programs which need to read dBase data.

Software products themselves are rarely static entities that do not change. Instead, they undergo periodic upgrades to better match the needs of users. dBase and R:Base have shown this evolution in their own releases. The first releases of dBase II were decidedly not "user friendly." Instead, they greeted the user with a dot on the screen. The commands were in the manual. Yet dBase contained a programming language that let the sophisticated user construct custom programs for others that hid the dot-prompt origins of dBase completely from the user.

R:Base, on the other hand, has always paid specific attention to neophyte users. Not only were new users originally helped carefully along the way to creating a data base, with very little effort on the user's part, but R:Base could construct custom entry screens and other niceties that made dealing with the program much easier than dealing with that dot in dBase. But it had no programming language.

Yet with subsequent releases, what happened? Suddenly, dBase III and III+, and dBase IV constructed sophisticated user interfaces and assist modes that equalled those found in R:Base. And R:Base not only improved on its own strengths, but developed a programming language of its own. Thus the two programs are still gravitating toward each other as they both become more sophisticated. To those familiar with both programs, their influence on each other is obvious and, for the most part, welcome.

Yet dBase has maintained its status as the dominant player in the MS-DOS data base market. The effect of this success snowballs as more and more literate users learn how to manipulate dBase file structures and even program in the dBase language. Job applicants are statistically more likely to know dBase than R:Base, more likely to know Lotus 1-2-3 than Supercalc, more likely to know WordPerfect than XyWrite III.

## DBMS RECOMMENDATION

Your requirements for a dbms may vary, but we suspect they won't vary by much. From the discussion above it may be obvious that we are fans of dBase. We are, particularly of the file structure itself, both from a development standpoint and from that of a user. Yet dBase is expensive, overpriced, and the company itself has been accused of a certain arrogance born of success. They think they own the language.

We do not think dBase would be a clear winner in this regard if it were not for the vast support network which has grown around dBase. The same sort of network simply has not materialized for other dbms systems, no matter how good they are. Compilers, clones, and add-ons to dBase often hit the best-seller lists themselves.

If you were to compare dbms systems feature by feature, our guess is Paradox would win more times than not. Paradox 386 is especially attractive from a technical standpoint. There are lots of things it will do that dBase won't. Of course, it is designed for a 386 processor, so you won't be able to take advantage of it on any installed base of pre-386 micros.

Paradox 3.0, however, has no such restriction, and it received top reviews every time. InfoWorld rated it 9.5 out of 10 in their latest survey (1-8-90), far ahead of the competition, including the dismal dBase IV at 4.0.

The biggest reason dBase IV received such a low score appears to be the long list of bugs in the first release. The reviewers stated it would have earned up near Foxpro (7.7) had the bugs not been present.

The biggest issue, however, is that Paradox does not have a large installed base, a large after-market, and a trained army of programers. From a use standpoint, dBase or Paradox will hold your hand if you want it to, or free you to become as creative as you would like. We will readily concede Paradox, or any other dbms, is "the best," but we worry about the person who is next in line for the job. Is he or she likely to know Paradox or dBase? I'm sorry, but the answer is obvious.

We believe it is important to use and understand the dBase structure in particular, but you can do this with Wordtech's DBXL or Foxbase Pro just as easily as you can with dBase itself. The mail order price for DBXL is not much over $100, compared to $400 for dBase, or $795 if you insist on paying full retail. Foxbase, unfortunately, has a dBase price ($795). One way or another, we recommend you learn a dBase-compatible language as an excellent general-purpose tool. There is a vast pool of support out there, and you will never be alone.

DBXL is particularly attractive for several reasons. Not only is it an extension of dBase itself, it also dovetails nicely with Wordtech's other major product: Quicksilver. This is a dBase compiler that can turn dBase code into a stand-alone application which does not require dBase to run. If you have the same program that must be run on several machines, this is a nice way to circumvent multiple copies of the original applications program.

Wordtech has also recently signed agreements with Oracle, a mini and mainframe data base company which is highly regarded. This alliance should prove beneficial to both Wordtech and Oracle. It means that eventually you will see DBASE at the mini and mainframe level, supporting standardized interfaces and backed by large companies.

In summary, then, Foxpro does better at dBase than dBase itself, and Wordtech's DBXL is a good clone alternative which is much cheaper and allows instant interfacing to a compiler like Quicksilver.

Now, having picked our favorites, there is no reason why you can't go elsewhere. If you just have to have R:Base or Q&A, go ahead! Just hope the person who takes your job after you leave knows it as well.

## COMPILERS

One of your alternatives for data base systems may involve compilers. Compilers can take your programs and compile the code into machine language. This means the intermediate step of interpretation is lost. The resulting executable file has the potential for several advantages. They involve speed, integrity, and cost.

Compilers, generally speaking, are faster than the languages they replace. Machine language code, of course, is about as low as you can get in the language hierarchy. There are no intermediate steps.

The second major advantage to compilation is integrity of the code. It is a rare person who can jump into a compiled application (runtime code) and change the way it works. With dBase code (source code), however, this is fairly easy to do, and to mess up. Whether this is an advantage or disadvantage depends on the side you are on.

If you are the compiler, rather than the compilee, you don't want just anyone changing things around. We have an accounting system that is in place at several libraries, a park department, and a fire department. We furnish source code. But if our friends using the program decide to change something, how can we support it?

We can't. It's not so bad if they change a line on a screen, or take the dashes out of the middle of a postcard, but if they change some program logic, there is no way we can follow what they have done, particularly when we are attempting to make all programs uniform for all sites.

The bad side of all this is that it costs us more to support a program if we insist on doing it in this manner. We have taken control away from the site, out of fear, mostly, and placed the entire responsibility for running the show on our own shoulders.

The third advantage of compilers is that you can purchase only one copy of dBase, or whatever dbms is your favorite *and* (a crucial point) has a compiler for it, write a program using that file structure, and distribute as many copies as you like without buying new systems.

## SPREADSHEETS

The spreadsheet arena is not much different from that of data base systems. Lotus 1-2-3 is the market leader. Until recently, there weren't any pretenders to the throne. That may be changing as other major software companies are pushing hard to overtake the dominant Lotus. Ironically, it is some of the Lotus clones that are making the largest penetration of market share.

Lotus began life as an improved version of Visicalc, the software product that made the world notice the Apple II as something other than just a game computer. Although initially successful, Visicorp, the maker of Visicalc, made a series of strategic marketing errors.

First, they refused to write a version of Visicalc for CP/M machines, the early alternative to Apples which thrived in the 8-bit microcomputer world. Instead, Supercalc was written for these machine by another firm. Largely a knock-off of Visicalc (the command structure had perhaps three commands different than Visicalc), it enjoyed immediate success in that realm.

Second, as the computing world's attention shifted away from the Apple II to the newer IBM 16-bit machine, Visicorp again failed to capitalize on the shift. Instead, on of its former employees took the winnings from selling his Visiplot graphics program to Visicorp to found Lotus Development Corporation. Meanwhile, Visicorp embarked on a disastrous operating system development program which failed miserably. Soon, Visicorp faded from site.

Lotus 1-2-3 did not. Showing clear origins in Visicalc, Lotus 1-2-3 added graphics and severely limited data base functions to those of the spreadsheet (thus the "two" and "three" of 1-2-3) to become the dominant spreadsheet for the IBM. Since that happened, no other spreadsheet has come close to dominating this field. This has allowed Lotus to make a few mistakes and survive, the way Visicorp could not. The introduction of Symphony, originally conceived as a 1-2-3 replacement, has never materialized to the extent the developers had hoped. The Lotus word processor, Manuscript, has met a similar fate.

Lotus 1-2-3 has changed, too, over the years, but not by much. Release 3 is out there now. And although accounts are favorable, it looks like their "other" release, 2.2, is outselling its big brother. Release 2.2 isn't really much different than Release 2.01. The "most changed" features are in the programming arena, little invoked by casual users.

Release 2.01 was not much different than Release 1A, except for some esoteric file structure changes that succeeded only in making users angry. It was better at managing memory and a few other things, but not that much different. If anything, it suffers from creeping featurism—there are just more of the same things. Supercalc was translated to run on IBMs, then enhanced, but it simply has never caught on as 1-2-3 has. Yet its graphics functions are much better than those of Lotus. Contex MBA, an original competitor that was actually first to the market, has also faded from view.

It's interesting that 2.2 is outselling 3.3. The reason is largely because 3.0 requires a larger computer. It wants at least a megabyte of RAM, and it would surely like an AT or better. The installed base of micros is about 50 million now, most of them MS-DOS machines. They are standard 640K machines that do not have extended memory. Lots of them are running Lotus 2.01. People may convert to 2.2, but they can't convert to 3.0 because it won't run.

Ironically, Quattro, by Borland International, publishers of Sidekick, Superkey, and the Turbo series of languages, has made a stab at Lotus' domination not by attempting to improve greatly on the product Lotus publishes, but by emulating it as exactly as possible without getting sued. As a low-priced alternative to Lotus 1-2-3 ($195 versus $495) Quattro has taken up the slack left as Lotus has failed to release Version 3.0 on time. Quattro Pro has received very favorable reviews.

Paperback Software's VP Planner and Mosaic's Twin are attempting a similar venture. Lotus has sued them both, but as of this writing nothing has come from this lawsuit posturing. It has been several years since the suits were first filed.

As the MS-DOS world moves away from PCs and even ATs to the 80386 realm and Windows, there will be another threat to Lotus: Microsoft's Excel. This newer spreadsheet requires a fast machine and enhanced graphics or it won't run at all. To all accounts, it is an excellent product. Microsoft's Multiplan, on the other hand, has never enjoyed overwhelming success for PC users.

Once again, the situation is similar. Because Lotus is dominant, other publishers are sure to at least import Lotus files. People are statistically more likely to know Lotus than a competing product. Indeed, this time the competitors are further behind than they are in the world of the dbms.

Yet Lotus, too, has been accused of arrogance. The last major software company to remove copy protection from its products, Lotus has also refused to sell to mail order dealers. The policy has since been rescinded, but they once went so far as to track down grey market dealers tracing serial numbers in an attempt to stop them from selling mail order. Because of its dominant position, Lotus has continued to grow, but this means that the price difference between Lotus and the clones is wider than it otherwise would be.

## SPREADSHEET RECOMMENDATION

In the first draft of this book, we had pretty well decided to recommend Borland's Quattro. It is enough like Lotus 1-2-3 that those who know it can adopt to Quattro easily. Blessed with better graphics and a more versatile interface, Quattro is also much, much cheaper. Borland, after all, started as a mail order business. It's prices are not as cheap as they once were, but they sell credible products reasonably.

Borland is also on better financial footing than any other software clone maker. They will likely be able to support the product for some time to come. As the industry moves into faster machines, Excel will be the spreadsheet to watch, especially if Lotus manages to release 1-2-3/G with a graphical interface. Expect to see the dBase/R:Base battle unfold once more as Lotus and Microsoft improve their products in an attempt to outdo one another in the future.

However, we have encountered a couple of difficulties that prevent us from making this recommendation today. First, Quattro does not handle the 1-2-3 macro language quite the same way 1-2-3 does. In one case, we pulled together a budget spreadsheet which works with macros to emulate pretty closely the uniform interface we described in Chapter Two. But Quattro began behaving erratically with this program, so much so that we have purchased a copy of 1-2-3 to replace it for this particular application.

The other major difficulty we encountered was with memory. Quattro does not have separate programs for graphics and the spreadsheet itself. As a result, it takes more memory at once. Our largest "mega-template" fits easily into 1-2-3 with memory to spare, but we cannot load it onto a colleague's machine running Quattro because it won't fit.

Therefore, rather reluctantly, we are suggesting Lotus 1-2-3 as the spreadsheet of choice. We recommend Release 2.2 specifically, not Release 3.0. Why? Because 2.2 will run on present-day machines. You don't need extra memory. Printing output has been enhanced greatly with the addition of the Allways printing utility program, and graphics have improved slightly.

If we were starting fresh with AT-class machines, we might try Excel as a good alternative. It certainly gets consistently rave reviews, and its hooks to the emerging Windows environment by the same publisher mean it is positioned for the future. Right now we hesitate, both because of the higher price and the fact that it requires a higher-priced machine to operate. We're watching this one closely; and so should you. In our opinion, Excel will be the only real competition to Lotus.

## WORD PROCESSING

The word processing market for MS-DOS is much more fragmented than that for spreadsheets or data base systems. The dominant firm is WordPerfect, selling a product of the same name. Other major firms are Micropro, publishers of WordStar, Microsoft with Word, Ashton-Tate with Multimate, and a host of others including XyWrite III, PFS: Professional Write, and PC Write.

Certainly in this realm any of the top word processors offer most of the features of the others. WordPerfect and Microsoft Word have been leap-frogging each other in features for a number of years. WordPerfect's latest Release 5.1 has incorporated graphics and a few other goodies which give it the top status currently. Indeed, it also compares favorably with desktop publishing packages.

Microsoft has followed suit. Word 5.0 has its roots in the typesetting world. Indeed, in earlier versions this orientation was much more obvious. It benefits from the use of a Mouse; and it has a dandy spelling checker and thesaurus included in the package. Its outline feature has improved with the last release. It is a very robust program. People who know it well (such as Peter Norton) claim it can be used as a desktop publishing program with excellent results.

XyWrite III has long been touted as the word processor for writers. It is noted at being extremely fast, though perhaps cryptic to use. It also can be customized to the user's desires. Wordstar was the original word processor in the CP/M days. It hasn't done as well in MS-DOS, after several tries.

Word processors lend themselves to file transfers perhaps more easily than some other types of software. The important thing to insist upon is that the product be capable of writing standard ASCII files to disk. With this ability, the resulting file can be loaded into any other word processor with ease, then formatted according to local custom.

In the word processing realm we are not as quick to make a recommendation. The stand-outs are still obvious, but there are many of them; and there is no particular reason to chose one over the other. We still suggest some semblance of standardization, but this time it is not out of some idea that one word processor is inherently better than another.

The real reason for standardization of software is not the product anyway. Instead, it is the resulting ease of translation between people, the spread of knowledge on how to use a product over many people, and the resulting easing of stress on the micro manager attempting to draw all the pieces together.

## WORD PROCESSING RECOMMENDATION

Any of those named above. They are all available for about $200 mail order and good values at that price. They will do most everything possible with a word processor. Successive releases will ensure you get the competitor's features on the next update anyway. WordPerfect has gained the largest following, to near cult levels. Purchasing a market leader such as this does not imply any lack of fortitude. It simply means you trust your fellow user.

For those who wish to save significant money, you might try PC Write. Why? Because it is free. Available through many user groups, the program has a very good reputation. As a "shareware" program, the deal is that you try it to see if you like it. If you decide PC Write is for you, you are requested to send in a registration fee of $75.00. This entitles you to a printed manual, updates, and support.

Borland has entered into the word processing fray with Sprint, a chameleon product much like Quattro. Sprint can emulate the command structure of any of the other major word processing programs on the market. Its retail price of $195 is not much different from the street price of most word processors. In this case, we do not recommend the clone alternative. The price savings garnered by doing so are not as great as within other arenas. Instead, get the real thing.

We use Microsoft Word. Since we have been with Word since Version 1.0, we're not likely to change. XyWrite might be marginally better; and any computer guru ought to at least know a little about WordPerfect, but Word works well; and it would take a major improvement in one of the others to get us to spend time learning a completely new interface for another program. It's just not worth it from the standpoint of efficiency.

## DATA COMMUNICATIONS

The data communications realm is becoming more and more important. Online data bases are full of useful information; and electronic mail is available around the country. Data communications alone will not overtax your computer. Indeed, even a dumb terminal will do. The more sophisticated data communications programs have a wide variety of error-correction protocols, buffer capture facilities, and even script languages. These features allow truly amazing feats to be accomplished through such a program. Your computer can call their computer in the dead of night when rates are low, automatically sign-on, download mail or information, and automatically shut-down again. Some of the programs can do all this in background while you're busy spreadsheeting in foreground.

One of the more tried programs in this category is Crosstalk XVI. Although since superseded by Crosstalk Mark IV, the earlier version seems still to be selling well. As programs go, this is relatively inexpensive, running at about $100 mail order. Crosstalk has a full array of features. You will not lack for purchasing this program.

Our clone candidates are many this time. Mirror III by Softklone emulates Crosstalk. The second version changed only the screen displays as a result of a copyright suit by the publisher of Crosstalk. The third version has moved further afield. Much cheaper in price, Mirror also allows you to run in background. It emulates all the commands of Crosstalk, and adds a few of its own.

PC-Talk III is another choice which has one clear advantage: It's free. Available on many public bulletin boards, it is a robust program which has most features of data communications packages. As a "shareware" package, if you like it, you are asked to send a registration fee to the publisher.

Procomm is another shareware program which is not 'free' according to the publisher. They ask for a registration fee if you use it. It has quite zippy screens, lots of features, and is used by lots of people. We have found Procomm to be very widely used. We have a dial-in to our online public catalog, and likely as not, if it's an MS-DOS machine dialing in, it is running Procomm. As a result, we have a copy just so we can talk people through the menu choices.

## SUMMARY

The applications listed above are not intended to be the ones that will fulfill your every need in data processing. They are general tools proven able to fulfill many different needs. They can be customized or used raw. Usually, they are either easy or difficult, depending on how you've set them up. In every case, we have suggested a proven market leader, or a robust clone that equals that market leader in performance, but is cheaper in price.

Certainly our recommendations are not the only choices available. We know that; and we've sprinkled that point in various ways throughout this discussion. Surely any PC Guru has already developed preferences. We see no problem with that. If you've decided Revelation is the slickest data base management system in existence, feel free. If Lucid 3D is your spreadsheet of choice, we're enthralled. Remember that you must be willing to support what you have selected. We maintain that some consistency over the organization will be beneficial to both you and your users.

If you find yourself resisting this approach, we understand that you have your reasons, just as we do. We offer some guidelines to help you choose your personal favorite for the organization. This will help you maintain your leadership role; and will make naive users look up to you for guidance. These guidelines will help to make you indispensable. They represent job security, at least for awhile.

1. **Make sure you choose software which is esoteric.** If it is published by a programmer working out of the corner of the bedroom, this would be ideal. We all know software is written best by one person alone at night. Visicalc was written by one person. dBase II was the result of one person's efforts. Even the core of 123 was written by one person. It also helps if the version you are using is not quite done. Also, be sure the programmer does not have a telephone number. In fact, it is preferable if she moves out of state, or dies.
2. **Make sure you are the only person who knows or can know how the software works.** "Undocumented commands" are a great help here. You can save people more often, and they will be grateful. Be sure no help screens are available for the program. It would also help if no books were published about the program.
3. **Make sure the data structure is cryptic enough to require specialized utilities.** A data base system, for example, should have no method to actually write reports. This must be done from within a programming language. If the language is "C"

instead of BASIC, it would be much better. That way you can design all the reports yourself.

4. **Be sure to sneer at any software package that is actually popular with anyone.** In fact, the more popular a software package is, the more copies it has sold, and the more market share it "owns," the worse it is. If a million copies have been sold, you can be pretty sure it isn't any good. If a large after-market of support programs, consultants, and clones have also sprung up around the product, rest assured it is very bad. If it weren't, why would all that support be necessary?

5. **Ideally, you should write all applications yourself.** Be sure to include hidden commands that will help you maintain the program. For example, in a payroll system, insert a command that must be typed in once every six months, or a small routine will be called that wipes out the entire hard disk past the point of recovery. If this routine used Norton's Wipedisk command with the /G option (to conform to government security specifications for erasing hard disks) this would be ideal. If your PCs are hooked to mainframe computers, the possibilities are even more inspiring.

6. **For custom applications, compile all the programs, then keep the source code hidden at home.** Any changes must go through you.

You can see that the application of even a few of these hints will go a long way to establishing a user-friendly environment in the work place, after they get rid of you.

# 4 CONFIGURATION MANAGEMENT

What is Configuration Management? It is a discipline in and of itself. To an engineer, configuration management has to do with the types of chips on circuit boards and how they are put together. To the military, it means which equipment is placed on which submarine. Our purposes are a little more sedate. Configuration Management to us simply means an ordered way of tracking just exactly what we have in the way of computers and peripherals.

If you have only a few computers, configuration management is usually inside your head. You know that the computer on Susan's desk has a Seagate 225, but the one on Joan's has a Miniscribe. You know which system, has 640K and which one has that special speed-up card from Microsoft. If you're paying attention, you even know which software is assigned to which machine, or at least which software is somewhere nearby.

But as your operation grows, PCs will be as common as telephones. But where telephone sets are all pretty much the same, PCs aren't. They look the same on the outside, but inside there are all those slots filled with different boards, and hard disks filled with different software. There are different keyboards, different printers, different ports, and different monitors. Some PCs have 360K drives and some have 1.2MB. Some may have three and a half inch disks. Some are hooked up to the mainframe; some stand alone.

And software. If you're unlucky, every manager in the place is using a different spreadsheet and a different favorite word processor. If they're feeling independent, they have different data base systems and communications products as well. Of course, they may have stolen some of their software from each other, willingly or not. Without copy protection, this is easy to do. Just don't get caught. Software publishers never go after individuals. It's not worth it. Instead, they go after corporations. They make such nice examples, and they may even have money.

If you are lucky, you have only an inventory problem. And that's what configuration management is all about.

Fortunately, now that you have all these neat software tools at your disposal, it should be easy enough to write a data base program which will work for you. But just in case, we've provided a program here to discuss. It is called PC Tender, a cousin to Member Tender, our organization management software and B.A.R.S. Tender, our accounting program. You may have PC Tender. Written in dBase and compiled with Quicksilver, it will run anywhere MS-DOS runs. It's part of the free disk offer at the back of this book. It is presented here as an example. It may not be exactly suitable for you, though we hope it is. It does not seek to capture every bit of information about your PCs, but will provide enough information so that you might at least know what you have in the field.

## INITIAL SETUP

The system is self-contained. All you have to do is copy the files onto an appropriate sub-directory of a hard disk on a typical MS-DOS machine. We suggest the sub-directory PCTENDER; and currently, if you wish to use the built-in back up system, this directory is assumed. If you take care of that sort of thing yourself, then any directory name will suffice.

The system is written in dBase. We have provided it two ways. The first way is compiled with a program called Quicksilver. This allows the program to run WITHOUT the dBase program itself. Therefore, if you do not own dBase, you do not need to purchase it in order to run the program.

The bad news is that you will not be able to change anything about how the program runs. You could write your own dBase code to access the data base of information itself, but this would requires circumventing the actual PC Tender program itself. If you find yourself needing to do this a great deal, then you might as well write your own program, with data elements more suitable to your needs.

We have also provided the source code, the actual dBase code that has been compiled. If you want to run the program with dBase, then these files must be used. You may use either dBase III+ or dBase IV. We have tested PC Tender with both programs; and it works with both programs.

The advantage of this approach is that source code is accessible to you and may be modified by you. You can change anything in the program, including the screens themselves, as long as you separately purchase the Saywhat!? screen generation program, detailed elsewhere in this book. The disadvantage, of course, is that you need to purchase dBase to do this.

## MAIN MENU

PC Tender's main menu has options for entering data on hardware, software, or peripheral devices such as printers. It also has options for reporting and editing. The Main Menu itself is shown in Figure 4.1.

Operation is straightforward, based on the Saywhat screen generation program discussed in the chapter on the Uniform Interface. Once PC Tender is run, a moving bar menu appears over

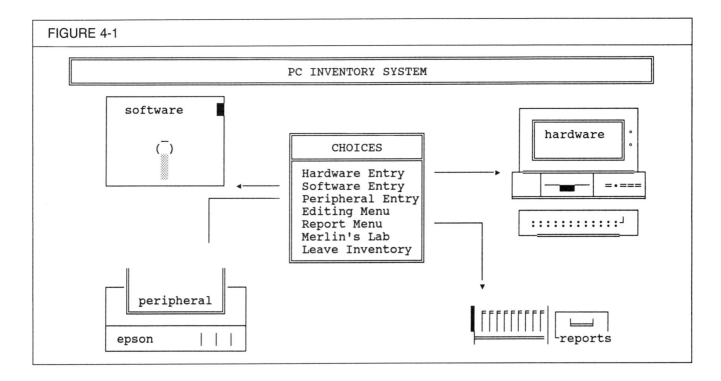

FIGURE 4-1

**FIGURE 4-1**
PC Tender Inventory Main Menu

the choices. Move the bar with the arrow keys and press [Enter] for your choice, or simply press the first letter. The next screen will pop into view.

Whenever you encounter a moving bar window, pressing the [Escape] key will move you backwards one choice, except for the main menu, where you must intentionally quit the program.

Because the moving bar initially rests on hardware entry, simply pressing [Enter] will take you to that choice. Figure 4.2 provides the basic input screen for hardware. The top portion of the screen is reserved for information about the unit in question; the bottom part is for what is inside the machine.

You must enter data in the first field. If you do not, the program assumes you made a mistake and want to return to the previous menu. Thus, pressing the [Enter] key here is just like pressing the [Escape] key. All other entries can be skipped, if desired.

An explanation of the intent for each field follows. As is usually the case with any "hard-wired" data base system like this one, you may choose to enter information differing from the original intent. There is very little error checking here, so you are not restricted.

**Brand Name:** is the name the manufacturers give their machines.

FIGURE 4-2

```
            *** PC INVENTORY ADD/EDIT RECORDS ***
```

| Brand Name:<br>Model Number:<br>Their Serial: | | Assigned To:<br>Location:<br>Our Serial #: | |
|---|---|---|---|
| Vendor:<br>Total Cost: | | Purchase Date<br>Record Number | |

| Drive Information | | | CPU Information | | Card Information | |
|---|---|---|---|---|---|---|
| | Type | Size | CPU:<br>Speed: | | Slot 1:<br>Slot 2: | |
| A:<br>B:<br>C:<br>D: | | | Power:<br>RAM:<br>Serial:<br>Parallel | | Slot 3:<br>Slot 4:<br>Slot 5:<br>Slot 6:<br>Slot 7: | |
| Type of Monitor: | | | | | Slot 8: | |

**FIGURE 4-2**

PC Tender basic hardware entry screen used for adding or editing data

You may or may not include the manufacturer here. We have an American Club 286. That entire phrase will fit in this location.

It's important to be consistent here. If you have more than one of the same type of machine, be sure to call them the same thing each time. Later on you'll want to know how many of each type you have. If you don't maintain this consistency, then the reporting programs will detail different listings for each variation.

**Model Number:** is their model number, not yours. Most models have some sort of designation; and if you ever need service, the repair shop will want to know exactly what you think you have. Most have numbers, but words are not uncommon. Our Club AT is an "1800i" under model number. There may be some esoteric information within the number (What's the "i" stand for, anyway?) so be sure to get it right.

**Their Serial:** is the serial number they place on their product, not the inventory control number you may place on yours. If you've filled out a warranty card, you must have this information anyway. Otherwise, look on the back or underneath. The serial number is probably on the same sticker as the model number.

Once again, their serial number is important. If they've made any changes not reflected in model numbers, they will be tracked by serial numbers. If the manufacturer discovers a faulty part, it will be tracked by serial number. There is likely an inborn date code within the serial number as well. In the case of a general recall on suspect equipment, serial numbers could save you money.

**Assigned To:** The person to which this micro is assigned. If you assign to departments, that would work here. But remember Pournelle's First Law of Micros: One Person, at least one CPU. One of the reports is printed by this field, so bear that in mind when making assignments here.

**Location:** Department, building, whatever. Where is it? There is also a report by location. Make sure locations are spelled the same way each time. Locations of "Central" and "CENTRAL" will be tabulated differently and print out as different locations.

**Our Serial #:** The inventory control number you place on the machine. Surely every large organization has an inventory control number these days. Governmental institutions require them. In our library, we have placed all hardware onto the circulation control system. Each PC has its own barcode, tied to a bibliographic record. Every type of PC has a record. Each copy is treated just like a copy of a book.

Your inventory control number can be anything you desire. Because of the way this system works, it is very important. It is probably best tabulated as a short number rather than a long one. This is because these numbers are unique; and they are the primary way in which the system keeps computers separate. Further, this number is also used in assigning peripheral devices and software to each computer system. You'll need to use these numbers in the editing function to pull out the particular computer you wish to edit and track.

**Vendor:** From whom purchased. Over time you will probably buy from several different vendors. This identifies who to call when it breaks, hopefully while the system is still under warranty. If you are purchasing a variety of machines over time, this will avoid any embarrassing moments of calling the wrong vendor to fix a warranty problem on a machine they did not sell you.

Tracking Vendor is also important in verifying contract disputes. Several times we have been in the unfortunate situation of having hardware which winds up not meeting hardware specifications as insisted upon in an RFP.

While you might suggest such things ought to be verified immediately, in real life this is somewhat more difficult. When several machines are involved which all look alike, it may seem reasonable to test one in order to pass them all. After all, getting them running is a small part of the battle. Now you have to load software onto them and get them to the field for impatient users.

Unfortunately, this may not show up the problem with a video card which is just slightly different on one machine compared to all the others. Only when you attempt to run a peculiar combination of software on the machine does the problem show up, often long after the bill has been paid.

But if you can prove such a problem, the vendor remains obligated to fix it. The sword over the head is the threat of no more sales, plus perhaps a publicity campaign among your fellow computer buyers to let them know of the problem.

**Total Cost:** For your records. Our first Apple II+ cost $4,000. Our last PC (with ten times more memory) cost $450. This field is particularly important if the machine has been purchased with grant funds, where such records are considered important.

**Purchase Date:** For your records. Amortization may be important if you are a private organization; not as much if you are public. In both cases, the date will help you argue for newer equipment. In conjunction with serial and model number, this date may be important with warranty claims.

We always put the date the equipment was placed into service as opposed to when it was ordered or delivered. You may also be able to use the date the bill was actually paid. This date must correspond with the date placed on any warranty card you may have sent to the manufacturer. In either case, stretching the warranty just a few days can prove beneficial.

We once had a Hayes 2400 baud modem with a two year warranty. It broke two weeks before the warranty expired; and Hayes replaced the modem with no questions at all when we sent it in.

**Record Number:** With this program the record number means the dBase record number. It is an internal control number used by dBase, provided here in case we need to drop down to dBase itself to ferret out a problem. These are assigned sequentially. They will stay the same always unless records are deleted, or the data base itself is sorted.

Because the record number is generated internally, it has no real value in itself. It is provided as a cross check and for those of you who delve around in dBase and want to understand the file structure.

## DRIVE INFORMATION

The next section is Drive Information. We've allotted four slots for drives. In our experience, it is a rare system that has more. If you do, you're probably being inefficient or are the victim of historical circumstances.

We want to know the type and the size. On our AT, we have the following information:

|    | Type     | Size   |
|----|----------|--------|
| A: | Generic  | 1.2 MB |
| B: | IBM PC   | 360K   |
| C: | Seag 251 | 40MB   |
| D: |          |        |

Here we have a judgment call to make. To many of you, drives are peripheral devices, often purchased separately from the computer itself. Should they not be listed as peripheral devices rather than in the body of the main listing?

If you would prefer, surely. Maybe both; you decide. We're particularly interested in brand names of the hard drives, and sizes of all drives. This is of obvious importance where only some machines can handle some formats.

We would offer a guess this will become increasingly important as the industry changes from five and a quarter inch drives to three and a half inch drives in the future. Only some machines will be able to handle both kinds of drives. Within each size format there is the further complication between 360K and 1.2MB (for five inch drives) and between 720K and 1.44MB for the three inch drives.

And you wondered why configuration management was necessary?

# CPU INFORMATION

The CPU Information details some of the internal specifications of your machines. Some of it may be useful in assessing your fleet of computers and determining what kinds of software may be appropriate for any given machine.

For example, Excel, the Microsoft spreadsheet, will only run with Windows. Further, it will only run on a 286 or better machine. (The Macintosh version is a different program altogether, of course). Most robust programs today are also pushing hard the 640K memory limitation of 8088 and 286 machines.

Expanded or extended memory may help here, we realize, But this all must be considered when assessing potential purchases. This program is designed to store and spit out the information necessary to that decision.

**CPU** is the type of processor. These days you will have an 8088, 80286, or 80386 for MS-DOS machines. 80486 machines may be out by the time you read this, but maybe not; and Bill Gates has just been officially talking about the 80586! The numbers will be different, of course, if you're using another type of machine altogether. We still have several early Apples (6502) and even a Kaypro (Z80).

This information is crucial for software compatibility, of course.

**Speed** may be important to you. For our clunker PCs, the speed is listed as 4.77 MHz. For the Turbos, it's 8 MHz. For the faster AT machines, the speed may be 10 MHz or 12 MHz. The newer 386 machines are running as fast as 33 MHz.

Speed alone will tell you very little. It's just another factor along with such things as drive access and transfer rates, speed of memory, and the particular speed of the video card you have which determines the "real" speed of the whole computer.

**Power** refers to the power supply. The earliest PCs had a power supply of 63.5 watts. This wasn't really enough to handle hard disks and other plug-in components. XT machines had power supplies in the neighborhood of 135 watts. Today 150 watts is common; and 200 watts is not out of reason.

Why is this important? Because if you're planning on adding a hard disk to a machine which was not originally purchased with one, then the power supply had better be adequate to the task.

It is true we have seen hard disk machines with 63.5 watt supplies. And they worked. The proper name for this activity is "tickling the dragon's tail."

Good luck. You'll need it.

**RAM:** is the amount of memory available to the machine. Most PCs have a limitation of 640K, though that can be exceeded, depending on the machine and the software.

Beginning with the AT two new memory schemes were introduced which managed to extend memory beyond the 640K barrier. Unfortunately, the terminology concerning this has become muddled, therefore it is difficult to keep the two schemes straight.

The first is called "Extended memory" because it extends beyond the 640K barrier up into the stratosphere, if necessary. It is an extension of the so-called "memory map" which is really memory above 1MB, not just 640K.

Extended memory is good for relatively little, in our view. It can be mapped for use as a super-fast disk drive located in memory instead of on a disk. It can also be used as a print-spooler to absorb print output into memory before it has a chance to actually be printed. And extended memory can be used as a cache to hold oft-used information from the drives to make the computer appear to move faster than it actually is.

But what it cannot do is be used for program information, either for the program itself, or for the data. This is reserved for "Expanded memory," which works a little differently.

With expanded memory, a small 64K chunk of memory is opened up from within the normal 1MB space allotted. This 64K is a window through which several pages (up to 8MB), each 64K long, can be channeled. It is done through a device driver called EMM.SYS that is addressed, like all device drivers, from within your CONFIG.SYS file.

If the software allows it, expanded memory can be used for data and programs. Examples of programs that use expanded memory include Lotus 1-2-3, Microsoft Word, Ventura Publisher, and Publisher's Paintbrush. There are many others.

Further complicating matters, you can turn extended memory into expanded memory; and some software is now capable of using extended memory directly.

**Serial** refers to the serial ports. Just a number here referring to the number of serial ports you do have. We suggest at least two for each machine, particularly in a large environment that may allow communication with a mainframe or mini.

One of the serial ports will be taken up by the hook to the mini. The other could be used for a modem, or perhaps a mouse, since so many now come in serial versions. There are a number of Local Area Network schemes that also use a serial port.

If you do not have a sufficient number of ports, then you will need to resort to cumbersome A/B switches to manage the cable mess you will have in back of your machine. This will likely be more expensive than simply buying another serial port for your machine.

**Parallel** refers to parallel ports. Used most often with printers. Once again, the software is looking for a number.

These days most printers are parallel printers. Occasionally, another type of device will run off a parallel port. Also, many video cards, in the older IBM tradition, come with a parallel port in addition to one likely to be on a multi-function card.

In our experience, the need for more than one parallel port is rare. Therefore, we do not recommend going out of your way to secure additional parallel ports. They're usually not necessary, unless you have more than one printer hooked up to a single machine.

**Type of Monitor** is the last item in this section. Just list it, along with the type. Is it an EGA? Monochrome? CGA? And what color screen is it? Some of this information will be available in the slot information detailed below. This is intended for the monitor itself.

Once again, you may prefer to add a monitor as a peripheral device. Your choice, but you may want to give a brief listing here anyway. That way, it will appear on the major print-outs.

# SLOTS

The last major category is labeled "Card Information." It is fair to say that most major microcomputers have slots in the back, into which you can plug various peripheral devices. Slots mean versatility. IBM copied Apple in this regard. Ironically, Apple closed up the early Macs, though newer ones, too, have slots in the back.

Although we've heard of PCs with more than eight slots, they're very rare. We saw one with twelve slots, but it was very expensive, intended primarily for the Local Area Network (LAN) market.

We've provided eight slots to fill in. Here you should place the various add-on cards, including the brand name and a brief description of what it does.

As you probably know, slots vary in their configuration, i.e.: Some slots are intended for certain types of cards. The biggest difference is between PC slots and AT slots. (ATs are the faster MS-

DOS computers that use a 286 or faster chip.) The PC slots have fewer connection points, hence the slot itself is shorter. AT slots have a larger number of connection points, therefore a longer slot. Actually, the short part of the slot is the same as the PC slots. Only the extension is different. However, some of the PC boards won't fit in the longer slots. They protrude into the space now taken by the extension.

Most manufacturers will provide at least a couple of PC slots to accommodate the older boards. Other than this extension, the slots are usually interchangeable.

Except for the 32-bit slots on 386 machines. Here we enter an entirely different realm. The 386 machines can take a vast amount of memory, mostly on extra boards which look very much like normal expansion boards. However, the new boards are even longer than AT boards; and they have more connection points to accommodate the wider data path (32 bits instead of 16 bits) which is handled by the 386 machines. Further, all these new memory schemes are proprietary, therefore the 32 bit slots will only take boards from the original manufacturer.

We bring this point up not with the intention of explaining every detail of the new boards, but to warn you that the proclamation of "8 slots" may include the proprietary slots which are of no use to the normal boards.

Plan accordingly.

A typical entry might be as follows:

        Slot 1: Hercules mono/LPT1
        Slot 2: Hayes 2400 internal
        Slot 3: Scanner interface HP
        Slot 4: Disk controller/COM2
        Slot 5: Hard disk control
        Slot 6: Memory 2MB/COM1:
        Slot 7:
        Slot 8:

## SOFTWARE

What kind of magic box you have and what kind of cards stuffed in it is only half the problem of managing the fleet. The other half is the software itself. Indeed, a rough guideline would be to plan on spending as much for software as you spent on hardware for each machine. The PC Tender program assumes software is part of the deal, allowing you to enter software packages at the time you enter hardware, or afterwards. Each software package is tied to the hardware on which it runs, that is, it is assigned to a specific machine.

Figure 4.3 shows a data entry screen for software. When you choose to enter software immediately after entering the hardware, this screen overlays the hardware entry screen, i.e.: it appears right on top of the information you just entered. If you choose to enter the software separately, this screen appears alone, with one added field for the hardware serial number.

**Name** is the name of the package, of course. The name of the publisher is often included in the name, such as Microsoft Word, but just as often is not, as in Publisher's Paintbrush.

**Version** can sometimes be a little difficult. Publishers are fond of discussing Redundo Word II, Version 5.1. Is the version "2" or "5.1"? We vote for 5.1, but use your own judgment. The "2" in the name ought to be part of the name itself. Often the syntactical construction of the name will help in identifying just how it ought to be segmented.

A problem can develop with version numbers when the publisher opts for the policy of "continuous revision." This is true with WordPerfect, for example. Although version numbers of those packages sold today are labeled "WordPerfect, Version 5.1" internally, the program is slightly different, depending on when you purchased the software, or how long the package has been languishing in someone's basement warehouse.

The only way you can tell what version you really have is by looking at the date on the program files themselves on the distribution disks! WordPerfect policy is to immediately replace defective disks, but only if you call them up with a problem that can be attributable to a bug fixed in a later version.

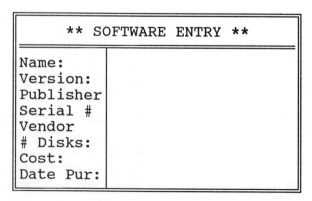

**FIGURE 4-3**
PC Tender's Software Entry screen.

**Publisher** is obvious. However, with mergers and acquisitions, the publisher often changes. Ashton-Tate bought Multimate; Borland bought Ansa. There are others.

**Serial Number** is for the number on the disks themselves. We keep track of this for several reasons. First, it is a good idea to send in registration cards for software. Not only are you then on the mailing list for future updates, you are also there for support, if any, and for bug fixes. Because software is rarely protected from copying any more, you may find yourself in a position of needing to prove you actually purchased the software.

Serial numbers are also the only way you can track copies of the same piece of software. Like it or not, the copyright and licensing provisions of software usually restrict it to one machine. If you have ten machines, you're supposed to purchase ten copies of Redundo Word, not one and make ten copies.

Some software is sold with a site license, legally allowing you to make as many copies as you wish. That information would go here as well. Instead of serial number, you could just write "site license."

We have noticed a trend away from serial numbers on software in the last couple of years. Instead, registration is taken from the post card itself; and updates are sent out based on these cards. This simplifies the process for the publisher, but may make individual tracking for your organization more difficult.

By **Vendor** we mean the place that sold you the software. We tend to skip around for the best price. This may or may not be important later on. We have found the best use of it is to track payment for the software in case of a later question.

**Number of disks** may or may not be important to you. It gives you an idea of the depth of the program. And this is supposed to be an inventory program, after all. For extensive programs that take ten or more disks, we purchase plastic disk holders for each copy of the program. We can count the number of copies of the program easily just by counting the number of disk boxes. This also makes the updating procedure much easier.

**Cost and date purchased** are also fields. Cost is summarized on many of the reports. Coupled with Vendor information, you can easily assess the best cost to the organization.

Date purchased is important for updating. Many publishers "pre-announce" their products and updates, primarily to attempt an advantage over creeping competition. Lotus' pre-announcement two years before shipping Release 3, for example, was made in an attempt to keep users from jumping to one of the other spreadsheet packages such as Excel.

Users who purchase an old version of a product after these pre-announcements may be eligible for a vastly reduced upgrade fee when the product finally ships. For example, we have several copies of dBase by Ashton-Tate. The one we purchased after the "official" announcement of dBase IV cost a mere $30.00 to upgrade. Previous copies of dBase III+ cost $175 to upgrade.

Considering the $695 retail cost of a new package, both were good deals, especially since Ashton-Tate was willing to upgrade very old copies of dBase II (not III) for the same $175.

If you add software at the same time you add machines, the machine serial number will be automatically added to the record. If you add software separately, then you will need to add the machine number manually. A printout of machines will give you the necessary information.

There is no limit to the number of software packages that can be attached to a machine. However, software reports will still print "together" so that you can tell how many packages of one product you own.

## PERIPHERAL DEVICES

Peripheral devices in this program are treated very much like software. We don't want a separate machine report for a printer. Although we have managed to attach printers to more than one computer at a time, the printer still must be reasonably close to at least one computer. The same is true with other peripheral devices such as modems, plotters, or scanners.

For the purposes of the program, then, a peripheral device must be associated with a computer.

The fields for peripheral devices are very similar to software.

**Brand:** means the manufacturer of the device. If it's a printer, it might be an Epson or Okidata, If it is a scanner, we suspect it's from Hewlett-Packard.

**Our Ser:** means the serial number for the piece of equipment that your organization uses to track such things. Software can usually get away without one of these bureaucratic stickers, but it's a fair bet a piece of hardware will not.

**FIGURE 4-4**
PC Tender's Peripheral Entry screen

```
┌─────────────────────────────────────┐
│        ** PERIPHERAL ENTRY **        │
├──────────────┬──────────────────────┤
│ Record #     │                      │
├──────────────┼──────────────────────┤
│ Assigned:    │                      │
│ Brand:       │                      │
│ Model:       │                      │
│ Serial #     │                      │
│ Vendor:      │                      │
│ Cost:        │                      │
│ Date Pur:    │                      │
│ Location:    │                      │
│ Our Ser #    │                      │
└──────────────┴──────────────────────┘
```

**Model:** Just as software has a version number, hardware devices have model numbers which change just as often. Printers are notorious for this, but other devices sport marginal improvements and new model numbers all the time.

Just as the case with hardware, the model number is probably found on the back of the device on the same sticker as the serial number.

**Vendor:** is the vendor from which you purchased the product, just as with hardware and software, and for the same reasons.

**Cost:** Your cost, for the same reasons, also.

**Date Purchased:** Especially valuable for warranty claims, date purchased also aids in tracking payment. It won't help you in getting upgrades. Unlike software publishers, hardware manufacturers don't care.

**Assigned:** means the person or department where the device is located.

**Location:** is the physical location of the device.

You may enter peripheral devices at the point you enter hardware, or separately, just as with software entry. As with software, there is no limit to the number of peripheral devices which can be assigned to one computer.

## SEPARATE SOFTWARE AND PERIPHERAL ENTRY

The Main Menu's first choice is for hardware entry. As explained above, software and peripheral devices can be entered automatically immediately after entering hardware into the system.

However, both these items can be entered separately as well. Software is the second menu choice and peripheral entry is the third choice from the Main Menu.

If either choice is selected, the appropriate screens appear to allow entry. the only difference is that now the screen asks you for your serial number of the hardware to which this software or this peripheral device is to be assigned.

The best way to find this information is from inventory printouts where all the information is provided. All the printouts which cover hardware have the serial number on them.

If you do not have the serial number of the hardware available, you can enter the rest of the information anyway, then add the serial number assignments at a later time.

**FIGURE 4-5**

Editing Menu is accessible from the Main Menu

**EDITING**

Choice number four from the Main menu is Editing. Editing allows you to change information in any of the three major categories:

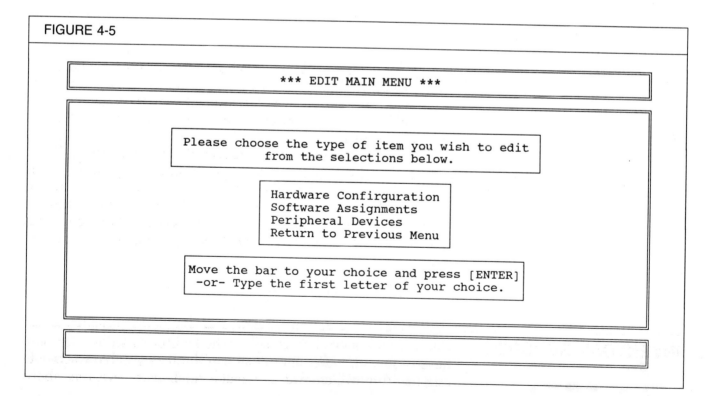

FIGURE 4-5

```
                   *** EDIT MAIN MENU ***


        Please choose the type of item you wish to edit
                   from the selections below.


               Hardware Confirguration
               Software Assignments
               Peripheral Devices
               Return to Previous Menu

        Move the bar to your choice and press [ENTER]
         -or- Type the first letter of your choice.
```

hardware, software, or peripheral devices. Choosing this takes you to a second editing menu, shown in Figure 4.5 below. The first task is to choose whether you wish to edit a record for hardware, software, or peripherals.

To be prepared, also have on-hand printouts of the database. You'll need them to choose record numbers attached to the information you wish to edit. This is admittedly more cumbersome than an elegant online approach, but the program is free, so no apologies.

Because you may be interested in editing a particular software record regardless of the hardware to which it is attached, access is direct to that record, via the record number you will find on the printouts. This will be particularly useful when you discover you've called a single package by more than one name. You'll need to "go direct" in order to edit to a uniform title.

**FIGURE 4-6**

The simple "finder" screen allowing access to previously entered records.

```
To Whom is this PC assigned?
_____
Name:
```

Figure 4.6 shows the brief record number entry screen. Once you type this in, the now-familiar screen for the record will appear, allowing you to change any of the fields within it.

For every choice you make the program will ask whether the information has been entered correctly; and if so, if you wish to edit any more records. Depending on your answers, the program will loop back to the appropriate location or take you back to the most recent menu.

In cases of data entry, when the record entered is new, a "null" entry in the first field will take you immediately back to the previous menu. In the case of editing a record, this is not true. If you call up a record in error, you will need to page through every field in order to "get out" back to a more familiar menu. This is done, of course, to allow you to edit any field, not just the first one.

**INVENTORY REPORTS**

Unless a sticker on a machine for the auditor to see is your only purpose, an inventory isn't much good unless you have accurate reports from which you can make intelligent decisions about

**FIGURE 4-7**
PC Tender Reports Menu

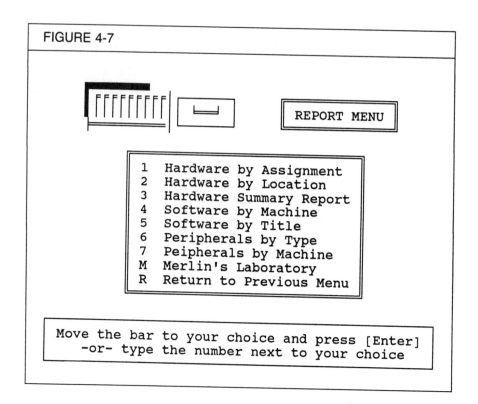

FIGURE 4-7

```
                    REPORT MENU

        1  Hardware by Assignment
        2  Hardware by Location
        3  Hardware Summary Report
        4  Software by Machine
        5  Software by Title
        6  Peripherals by Type
        7  Peipherals by Machine
        M  Merlin's Laboratory
        R  Return to Previous Menu

   Move the bar to your choice and press [Enter]
     -or- type the number next to your choice
```

equipment, to throw pieces away, ensure compatibility, or, in the case of a larger institution, just see what you have.

Choose Report Menu from the Main Menu to travel to that section. Figure 4.7 shows the report menu. The most comprehensive reports available from this system concern hardware. The first two choices in this Report Menu are exactly the same in content, but they are sorted by Assignment (Who has it?) or by Location (Where is it?). Figure 4.8 shows a typical page from this report.

All the information stored about each individual computer is presented here. At a glance you can tell exactly what is inside a computer and what its capabilities are. It is very similar to the initial hardware data entry screen introduced above.

The Hardware Summary Report, number three on the menu and shown in Figure 4.9, is a less ambitious report designed to give you an overview of PCs at a glance. It is currently ordered by assignment.

The Software Inventory Report (Figure 4.10) comes in two flavors: By Machine and by Title, corresponding to choices four and five.

**FIGURE 4-8**

PC Tender Inventory Report for hardware

```
FIGURE 4-8

PC INVENTORY REPORT - by assignment   ADMINISTRATION
--------------------------------------------------------------------
   Record Number:        12
   Assigned To:    ADMINISTRATION
   Location:       ADMIN (NORMA)
   Our Serial #:   3-9357-00527-7420
   Purchase Date:    / /
--------------------------------------------------------------------
   Brand Name:     CLUB AT           CPU:      80286
   Model:          1800i             Speed:    10 MHz
   Factory Serial: 10088             Power:    200 WATT
   Vendor:         KITSAP COMPUTERS  RAM:      640K
   Total Cost:        0.00
--------------------------------------------------------------------
   Serial Ports:  1    Parallel Ports:  2
--------------------------------------------------------------------
   Drive A:   CLONE      Size:  360K
   Drive B:              Size:
   Drive C:   SEAG 225   Size:  20 MB
   Drive D:              Size:
--------------------------------------------------------------------
   Slot 1:     MONO/LPT1        Slot 5:     HARD DISK CONTROLLER
   Slot 2:                      Slot 6:     FLOPPY CONTROLLER
   Slot 3:     COM1/LPT2        Slot 7:
   Slot 4:                      Slot 8:
--------------------------------------------------------------------
   Monitor Type:   MONO AMBER LEAD TECH
--------------------------------------------------------------------
```

The Machine report tells what software is assigned to each machine. We find it very useful when determining what version numbers are available on a given machine. Frankly, it is also useful in determining what software does not belong on a given machine. Armed with this report, you know which programs to erase.

The Title report (Figure 4.11) summarizes the titles, bringing all copies together. This is useful for tracking version numbers, of course, and making sure you don't miss someone when planning for an upgrade.

The Peripheral Reports (Option 6 and 7, Figure 4.12) are of the same variety as software reports, by machine and by type. They allow you to tell what peripheral devices are assigned to each machine, or how many Okidata printers you really have. Together with the hardware reports, they give a complete picture of hardware within the organization.

# MERLIN'S LABORATORY

Merlin's Laboratory is a menu option that appears on the Main Menu and on the Reports Menu. It's major function currently is to allow changes in printer type styles. It also allows an easy method to backup the current directory onto floppy disks from within the

FIGURE 4-9

```
   Page No.     1
   01/09/90

                            HARDWARE SUMMARY REPORT

   BRAND              MODEL      LOCATION          ASSIGNED             BARCODE


   ** TOTAL COST    0.00
   CLUB AT            1800i      ADMIN (NORMA)     ADMINISTRATION       3-9357-00527-7420

   ** TOTAL COST 1700.00
   CLUB AMERICAN      210D       ADMINISTRATION    ELLEN NEWBERG        39357005277487

   ** TOTAL COST    0.00
   CLUB 386           316SX      Art Department    Central              3-9357-00527-7352
   KRL PC                        BAINBRISGE        PC BACKUP            3-9357-00527-5341
   CLUB 286           1800A      CE REFERENCE      HEALTH NETWORK       3-9357-00527-7370
   KRL PC                        CE REFERENCE      MICRO BACKUP         3-9357-00526-1804

   ** TOTAL COST 1533.00
   CLUB 286           1800A      CENTRAL           SANDY CARLSON

   ** TOTAL COST    0.00
   LEADING EDGE       D1         CENTRAL REFERENCE NEWSPAPER INDEX PJCT 3-9357-00526-1689

   ** TOTAL COST 1533.00
   CLUB 286           1800i      Central/TS        Jeanne Blair         3-9357-00527-2272

   ** TOTAL COST    0.00
   IBM                PC         CENTRAL/TS        TECH SERVICES WLN    3-9357-00526-2158
   IBM                PC         CENTRAL/TS        TECH SERVICES WLN    3-9357-00526-2034

   ** TOTAL COST  995.00
   CLUB PC/XT         110        Central           Public Area          3-9357-00527-7495

   ** TOTAL COST 1700.00
   CLUB AT            208/210    Central/TS        Michael Schuyler     3-9357-00527-7545

   ** TOTAL COST    0.00
   CLUB XT            110        HARRISON HOSPITAL HEALTH NETWORK       3-9357-00527-7388
   KRL PC                        PORT ORCHARD      MICRO BACKUP         3-9357-00526-6480
   KRL PC                        POULSBO           MICRO BACKUP         3-9357-00527-0235
```

**FIGURE 4-9**

PC Tender Hardware Summary report

program. In other programs we have written, it performs other tasks as well. Figure 4.13 shows the Merlin menu.

Choosing the printer options takes you to a second menu which depicts two printers, one Laserjet, the other an Epson dot-matrix printer. Moving the arrow keys will highlight one name or the other. The object is to choose your printer and press [Enter] or just type an "L" for Laserjet or an "E" for Epson.

This provides more choices than might first appear. Most dot matrix printers these days offer an Epson emulation, i.e.: they work on the same control codes as Epson printers do. Epson printers are dominant in the marketplace, therefore all software which supports printers supports Epson, just as we do here. Therefore, other printer manufacturers force their printers to print in condensed or large type using the same initiation codes as Epson printers do.

The Epson choice, then, takes you to another menu where you can choose which typeface your printer will be using. Figure 4.14 shows the Epson menu. You can see from the choices that you can choose a variety of styles to suit your needs. We suspect you will

**FIGURE 4-10**

PC Tender Software inventory report (by machine). Several of the fields on the report have been cut off.

FIGURE 4-10

```
Page No.      1
01/09/90
                                    SOFTWARE INVENTORY REPORT
                                          BY MACHINE


       REC # NAME              VERSION   PUBLISHER          PUB SERIAL #        DISKS VENDOR           DATE PURCH


** ASSIGNED TO MACHINE: 3-9357-00526-1689
       25 MICROSOFT WORD        3.1     MICROSOFT          34099-310-0927880         EGGHEAD?         03/00/00
       26 MS-DOS                3.2     LEAD EDGE/MICROSOFT                     2     EWSU LSCA        03/00/00


** ASSIGNED TO MACHINE: 3-9357-00526-1804
       27 LIBRARY TERMINAL EMU 1.0     GEAC               KITS861101          1     GEAC             03/00/00
       28 MS-DOS                3.3     MICROSOFT                              2     KITSAP COMPUTERS 03/00/00
       29 MICROSOFT WORD        4.0     MICROSOFT          034099-400-0023668 10     EGGHEAD          02/10/89
       30 DBASE IV              1.0     ASHTON-TATE        5481697-40         14     EGGHEAD          02/10/89
       31 MEMBER TENDER         1.0     SKYSOFT                                1     MICHAEL          02/10/89
       32 READABILITY           1.0     SKYSOFT                                1     MICHAEL          02/10/89


** ASSIGNED TO MACHINE: 3-9357-00526-6480
       41 TERMINAL EMULATOR     1.0     GEAC               KITS861101          1     GEAC             03/00/00
       42 MICRO BACKUP          12      GEAC                                   1     GEAC             03/00/00
       43 PFS FIRST CHOICE              SOFTWARE PUBLISHING                          EGGHEAD          03/00/00
       44 MS-DOS                2.1     MICROSOFT          HOT COPY                                    03/00/00
```

want to experiment with elite typestyle and with the condensed typestyle. The latter is especially useful in printing wide reports on narrow paper.

Before you choose any option (other than a Return out of the Menu) be sure your printer is turned on. When you do choose an option, your printer will normally move forward by one line, even though it may not print anything on paper.

Choose to test your printer to make sure the command has "taken" appropriately. The line, "This is a test" will appear three times, assuring that the desired change has taken place. As long as you do not turn off or otherwise change the printer, the configuration code will remain in effect.

Before you begin to print, press your Form Feed (FF) button to make sure the printer knows you're beginning at a new page. The configuration option has just used up at least one line of the paper, maybe more. The reports all assume you are beginning on a fresh sheet of paper.

The Laserjet option is similar, provided in Figure 4.15. Here the options are more limited; and they assume you have a Laserjet Plus or Laserjet II that has only a few built-in fonts. Here there is no

**FIGURE 4-11**

PC Tender Software inventory report (by title). Several of the fields on the report have been cut off.

```
 FIGURE 4-11

   Page No.    1
   01/09/90

                                    SOFTWARE INVENTORY REPORT
                                            BY TITLE

       REC # MACHINE #          VERSION   PUBLISHER        PUB SERIAL #        DISKS VENDOR            DATE PURCH

   ** TITLE: AVATALK
           21 3-9357-00527-7370           ELTEK                               1     KITSAP COMPUTERS   02/14/89

   ** TITLE: DBASE IV
           16 3-9357-00527-7370   1.0     ASHTON-TATE      5495775-42         14    ASHTON-TATE        02/14/89
           30 3-9357-00526-1804   1.0     ASHTON-TATE      5481697-40         14    EGGHEAD            02/10/89
           49 3-9357-00527-7420   1.0     ASHTON-TATE      0851747-32         14    ASHTON-TATE        02/01/89

   ** TITLE: DOS
           52 3-9357-00527-7352   3.3     Microsoft                          2     Kitsap Computers   03/30/89

   ** TITLE: FLASHBACK
           14 3-9357-00526-2034   1.0     INGRAM           2000303            1     INGRAM             06/20/88

   ** TITLE: GTALK
            5 3-9357-00527-2272   3.1     GEAC                                1     GEAC SITE LICENSE  11/01/86
```

elite typeface, so you're pretty well stuck with courier or condensed. You could choose a landscape condensed font. If you do this, be sure to change your printing from six lines per inch to eight lines per inch. This will ensure the reports will print properly on what amounts to "shorter" paper, because you're printing lengthwise.

Once you leave any of the printer menus, the program will return you to your previous menu, either the report menu itself, or the main menu.

## BACKUP

Merlin also has a backup choice. The choices within this menu are for a complete backup of the program and the data, or a backup of the data files only. In either case, the standard DOS Backup command is used. We are merely invoking it from within the program to make it easier for you.

Backup is assuming the program is in the PCTENDER sub-

**FIGURE 4-12**

PC peripheral report. Once again, several of the reporting fields have been cut-off. The report prints on fifteen inch wide paper.

FIGURE 4-12

Page No. 1
01/09/90

PC PERIPHERAL INVENTORY REPORT
BY TYPE

| REC # MACHINE SERIAL # | OUR SERIAL # | VENDOR: | LOCATION | ASSIGNED TO: | DATE PURCH |
|---|---|---|---|---|---|
| ** BRAND & MODEL: EPSON | RX-80 | | | | |
| 2 415009 | 3-9357-00525-4296 | COMPUTER CONNECTION | CENTRAL/TS | 39357005262034 | / / |
| ** Subtotal ** | | | | | |
| ** BRAND & MODEL: EVEREK | MN-200 | | | | |
| 3 3WN 22717 | 3-9357-00527-7396 | KITSAP COMPUTERS | HARRISON HOSPITAL | 39357005277388 | 02/10/89 |
| ** Subtotal ** | | | | | |
| ** BRAND & MODEL: GOLDSTAR AMBER | 1210A | | | | |
| 6 MB-8080-1348 | 39357005277479 | KITSAP COMPUTERS | ADMINISTRATION | 39357005277487 | 02/27/89 |
| ** Subtotal ** | | | | | |
| ** BRAND & MODEL: HITACHI | 1503S | | | | |
| 4 7001249D | 3-9357-00527-7404 | OMEGA DATA | HARRISON HOSPITAL | 39357005277388 | 02/10/89 |
| ** Subtotal ** | | | | | |

directory. If you wish to change this, it is possible. The program affected is called BACKUP.PRG. You can change it with any program editor. Of course, this assumes you are using the un-compiled version of the program.

If you're reading this book, we do not need to admonish you on the need for backups. Every time we read the typical backup admonishment, we just say, "Yeah, yeah," and keep going. But occasionally, when we crash a hard disk, we wish we'd paid better attention. There is a law of diminishing returns. We suspect a direct correlation between the frequency of backups and the amount you are willing to retype when you lose all your data.

## DATA STRUCTURES

The data structures for the various data bases involved in the program are presented below:
Structure for database: C:pchard.dbf
Number of data records: 20
Date of last update: 07/19/89

| Field | Field Name | Type | Width | Dec |
|---|---|---|---|---|
| 1 | BRAND | Character | 20 | |
| 2 | MODEL | Character | 10 | |
| 3 | HIS_SERIAL | Character | 20 | |
| 4 | ASSIGNED | Character | 20 | |
| 5 | LOCATION | Character | 20 | |
| 6 | OUR_SERIAL | Character | 20 | |
| 7 | CPU | Character | 10 | |
| 8 | SPEED | Character | 10 | |
| 9 | RAM | Character | 5 | |
| 10 | POWER | Character | 10 | |
| 11 | SERIAL | Character | 3 | |
| 12 | PARALLEL | Character | 3 | |
| 13 | DRIVE_A | Character | 10 | |
| 14 | DRIVE_ASIZ | Character | 5 | |
| 15 | DRIVE_B | Character | 10 | |
| 16 | DRIVE_BSIZ | Character | 5 | |
| 17 | DRIVE_C | Character | 10 | |
| 18 | DRIVE_CSIZ | Character | 5 | |
| 19 | DRIVE_D | Character | 10 | |
| 20 | DRIVE_DSIZ | Character | 5 | |
| 21 | MONITOR | Character | 22 | |
| 22 | SLOT_1 | Character | 20 | |

*(Continues on page 124)*

FIGURE 4-13. Merlin's Laboratory Main Menu, a feature of many of our dBase programs.

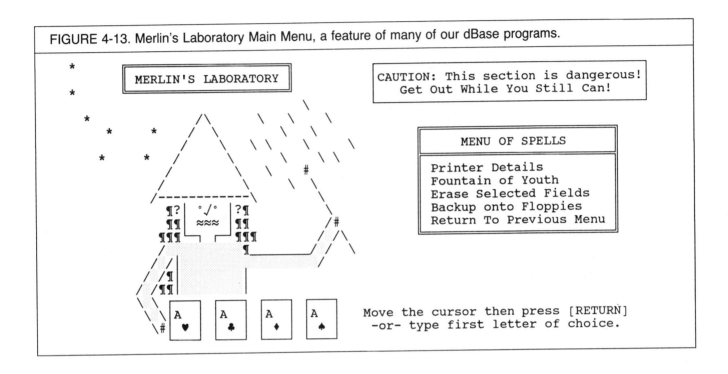

FIGURE 4-14. Menu to set printer options for an Epson.

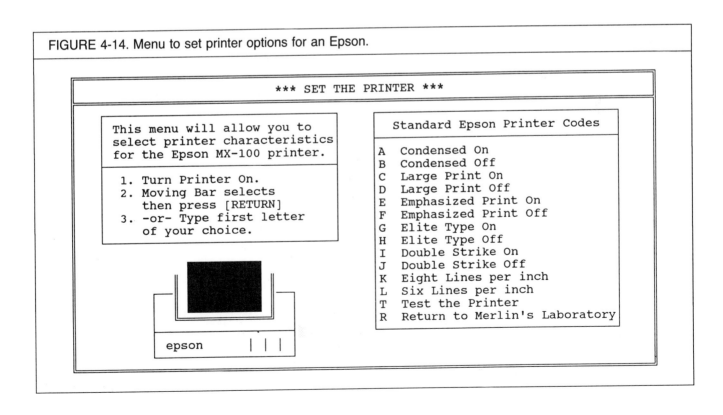

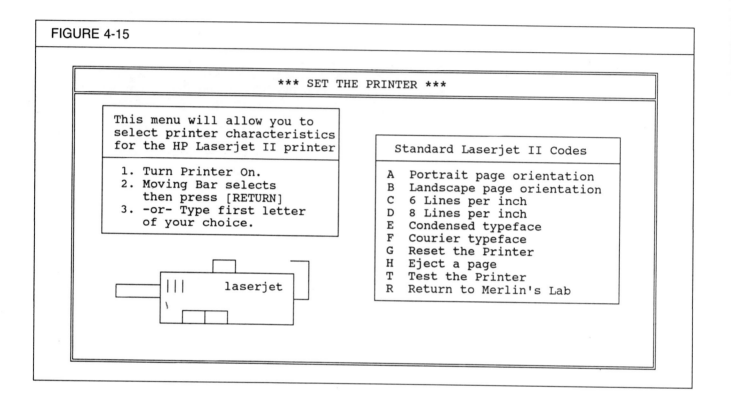

FIGURE 4-15

**FIGURE 4-15**

Menu to set printer options for the Laserjet

| Field | Field Name | Type | Width | Dec |
|-------|------------|------|-------|-----|
| 23 | SLOT_2 | Character | 20 | |
| 24 | SLOT_3 | Character | 20 | |
| 25 | SLOT_4 | Character | 20 | |
| 26 | SLOT_5 | Character | 20 | |
| 27 | SLOT_6 | Character | 20 | |
| 28 | SLOT_7 | Character | 20 | |
| 29 | SLOT_8 | Character | 20 | |
| 30 | VENDOR | Character | 20 | |
| 31 | COST | Numeric | 7 | 2 |
| 32 | DATE_PURCH | Date | 8 | |
| ** Total ** | | | 429 | |

Structure for database: C:pcperiph.dbf
Number of data records: 12
Date of last update: 07/19/89

| Field | Field Name | Type | Width | Dec |
|-------|------------|------|-------|-----|
| 1 | OUR_SERIAL | Character | 20 | |
| 2 | BRAND | Character | 20 | |

| Field | Field Name | Type | Width | Dec |
|---|---|---|---|---|
| 3 | MODEL | Character | 20 | |
| 4 | HIS_SERIAL | Character | 20 | |
| 5 | VENDOR | Character | 20 | |
| 6 | COST | Numeric | 7 | 2 |
| 7 | DATE_PURCH | Date | 8 | |
| 8 | ASSIGNED | Character | 20 | |
| 9 | LOCATION | Character | 20 | |
| 10 | HOST_SERIA | Character | 20 | |
| ** Total ** | | | 176 | |

Structure for database: C:pcsoft.dbf
Number of data records: 63
Date of last update: 07/19/89

| Field | Field Name | Type | Width | Dec |
|---|---|---|---|---|
| 1 | OUR_SERIAL | Character | 20 | |
| 2 | NAME | Character | 20 | |
| 3 | VERSION | Character | 10 | |
| 4 | PUBLISHER | Character | 20 | |
| 5 | SERIAL | Character | 20 | |
| 6 | VENDOR | Character | 20 | |
| 7 | DISKS | Character | 2 | |
| 8 | COST | Numeric | 7 | 2 |
| 9 | DATE_PURCH | Date | 8 | |
| 10 | HOST_SERIA | Character | 20 | |
| ** Total ** | | | 128 | |

## SOFTWARE UPGRADES

Managing software releases can be problematic. If you buy a car, you buy a certain model and year. If next year the auto manufacturer comes out with a new model, you get to trade your old car in at whatever market value you can procure for yourself, then buy a new car outright. That's how it works with most all products sold.

Except software.

Software changes over time for several reasons. User feedback inevitably requires the publisher to improve the product to meet rising expectations. Indeed, software sold at princely sums several years ago would be laughed off the market today. Users want state-of-the-art interfaces and problem-free operation. Word processing is a case in point.

The first word processor we learned was on a forty-column Apple II computer which would not display lower case letters on the screen. The program allowed the user to write via the computer; and a separate program printed out the results. Cryptic commands allowed the user to perform such elementary operations as change margins and set tabs. The total set of features was excelled by any typewriter around. The program would only hold a few pages of text before it would have to be cleared out. A document of any size was actually several documents chained together with special commands embedded in the documents themselves.

This word processor also had problems. Inexplicably it would stop running in the middle of a session. It would drop the computer back into a machine language monitor with strange numbers on the screen referring to the status of bit registers in the Apple's microprocessor. If you knew a few cryptic keystrokes (Escape-Shift-P-Return), you could get the computer back into the resident BASIC programming language. Then a machine language CALL statement (CALL -936) could sometimes allow you to jump back into the program. Usually, the only solution to recover was to turn the machine off and back on again, thereby reloading the program from disk. This only happened when the text buffer was nearly full, of course. Therefore, you lost the maximum amount of work possible.

But this was all such an improvement over loading the program from casette tape that it was tolerated for over a year. Besides, there was nothing else out there at the time.

Today the market leaders for MS-DOS are WordPerfect and Microsoft Word. The Macintosh has a substantial Microsoft Word following as well. Both these programs are robust, with literally hundreds of features. Both have an online dictionary and thesaurus. Both offer table of contents generation, outlining capability, mail merging, and indexes. Both run an astonishing variety of printers. They can chop text into separate windows, and they have an extraordinary number of commands to format text. WordPerfect is even available on mini and mainframe computers. Word works on IBM machines or the Macintosh. WordPerfect and Word both allow graphics to be incorporated within the text. Both programs can be used as rudimentary desktop publishing programs.

A problem with one of these programs is exceedingly rare. Indeed, support is necessary usually not because of program problems, but because users have a hard time absorbing the myriad of features available to them. And these are just two of dozens of similar programs, many of which have unique features which make them stand out in the marketplace. Surely none of these programs are perfect in every sense of the word, but perfection is becoming more a matter of preference than lack of widely-acknowledged features.

As of this writing, WordPerfect's latest version is labeled 5.1. Microsoft Word is also up to 5.0 and about to introduce a special Word for Windows, ordered by us, but not yet received. With each major release new features are added (and, without telling, bugs are fixed, and new ones introduced). The retail price usually stays about the same on these upgrades, though, of course, they tend to creep slightly upwards. Users of older versions are also allowed to upgrade for a nominal fee.

What is nominal? $50.00 is probably really nominal, but software publishers say nominal is anywhere from nothing to $400, depending. Minor releases are inexpensive. These are releases that have changes reflected in the numbering scheme past the decimal, i.e.: version 2.3 to 2.4. Major releases (e.g. 3.0 to 4.0) are usually a little more expensive, though you usually receive an entirely new set of manuals along with all new program disks.

Upgrade prices also depend on the length of time you have had a program. They are often free if you purchased an older version *after* the newer version was officially announced. Software publishers can play games with you here, too. When dBase IV was first announced with a July, 1988 shipping date, the offer was that if you purchased dBase III + before that time, the upgrade to dBase IV would be free. When July rolled past with no dBase IV in sight, the offer became an upgrade for $30.00. People who purchased dBase III + before the initial announcement would likely need to pay more than the $30.00.

A few years ago Ashton-Tate offered an even better deal. When dBase III was first released, they allowed users of any version of dBase II for any machine to upgrade for a nominal fee (the exact amount we have forgotten). Because we had purchased dBase II for IBM machines, as well as an earlier version for Apple II CP/M machines, we elected to turn in the Apple version for a new dBase III for IBM, thus retaining dBase II for the IBM as well.

It was once true that software publishers demanded you return a key disk and/or the original documentation in order to receive an upgrade. When Lotus 1-2-3 upgraded to Symphony, for example, users were required to buy an upgrade kit which included a mailer to return the original documentation as well as a copy protected key disk. Only then could you receive the new version of the software. Of course, Symphony never did replace 1-2-3 in the marketplace. Originally, they thought it would. Those who upgraded were often sorry they did. We were.

Today it is rare for a publisher to demand return of a key disk or the documentation. Software is rarely protected any more, and publishers do not care to bother with receiving tons of old documentation in the mail.

Instead, you get to keep the old version. In many cases, you are allowed legally to use the old version as well. We talked to representatives at Microsoft who informed us it was perfectly legal to upgrade to Microsoft Word 4.0, but keep older 3.1 versions around for use, as long as you kept them within the same organization.

The questions then become: Do you upgrade? Do you keep the older versions around? How does this fit into the configuration management scheme of things?

The initial upgrade question is not as easy as it sounds. You can easily upgrade into a new version of software that is more buggy and less accepted than the old version. This can happen with hardware as well, of course. Witness the slow start of IBM's microchannel architecture machines as users decided to wait or stick with the older varieties.

Lotus users who struggled with Symphony are another case in point. Initially conceived as a 1-2-3 replacement, Symphony has never caught on as well as initial company expectations. Instead, users stuck with 1-2-3, which then went through a major revision, and is about to undergo another. If you had upgraded to Symphony, you would have been stuck with it and, in this case, without the old documentation or disks to allow you to revert to the old program. For most people, upgrading to Symphony was a bad idea.

We are seeing the same phenomenon repeating itself with dBase IV, except this time there is a fundamental difference. dBase IV promises to be a major upgrade, just as dBase III was compared to dBase II. Users are already showing reluctance to upgrade. A hefty after-market has sprung up around dBase III, and the language has become a standard in the industry. Yet jitters over the upgrade have meant users are not buying anything. As a result several major after-market vendors have gone out of business. This includes Fox and Geller, for example, a well-known and respected provider of software to augment dBase III.

The difference, however, is that dBase IV is supposed to be able to run all dBase III applications. In other words, there is no penalty to upgrade if you have already written applications which work well in dBase III. Industry pundits have cast about rumors that compatibility is not one hundred percent, but this is typical.

We have had some experience in this arena. Our massive (to us) BARS Tender program, which operates our payroll, accounts receivable, and accounts payable, was written in dBase III (actually, the payroll portion was originally in dBase II). The programs all converted fine. One persistent problem related to the placement of decimal points in reports. Another problem surfaced with the use of the Saywhat!? screen generation program. dBase IV requires a slightly different method of popping up the screens. If it hadn't been for this last "anomaly" (as Ashton Tate likes to call them), very little conversion work would have been required. Even with this problem, the search and replace function in any word processor would make short work of the replacement code needed.

Our conclusion is that if you do not tend to "push" the language, everything converts. If you are constantly testing the outer limits of the program's capabilities, you'll probably encounter some problems. Of course, if you are capable of doing that in the first place, you ought to be able to figure out how to fix it as well.

If you just happen to have purchased dBase III just before the upgrade, you will wind up receiving two programs for the price of one. You won't have to turn in your old documentation or your old software. At $30.00 to upgrade, the move appears sound.

Some upgrades are minor in nature. Upgrading from Microsoft Word 3.0 to 3.1, for example, was a marginal proposition. With these upgrades, you may wish to hold off going through the effort unless there is a substantial added benefit. Software publishers will often add a program to the upgrade for a limited time to encourage such a move. Just after we purchased the Word Plus spelling checker for Microsoft Word, for example, Microsoft offered a cheap upgrade that included an improved version of this spelling checker. The upgrade wasn't a bad move for us; buying the speller days before the upgrade was.

In the final analysis, the upgrade decision will depend on the individual situation and market conditions. There is no pat answer.

Now, if you do upgrade, you may have the old versions lying around, complete with original documentation. Should you use these programs? Remember that we are seeking to get some consistency in operation across the board here. We don't want wide variations in performance and operation between programs, much less within programs.

We suggest that if you have enough money, everyone should be upgraded. If you need more copies, buy them. This will ensure consistency. You will not need to explain, "Well, if you're running 2.0 it works this way, but if you're using 3.0 it works this other way." This is not a minor consideration.

File structure is also a consideration here. If the upgrade changes the file structure, watch out. This happened when Lotus upgraded from 1A to 2.0. Users hated them for changing the structure. And it recently happened with WordPerfect from 4.2 to 5.0. In each case there were reasons for the change (particularly with WordPerfect), but the upgrade can be more stressful because of it.

In the case of WordPerfect, many outside vendors have written to the old file structure. Ventura Publisher, for example, has special ways to import WordPerfect files to that program. With the upgrade, this no longer works. As a result, Ventura and a number of other vendors have been forced to change their programs to accommodate this change. This sets off a flurry of patch disks to be sent to registered users to help them cure these new-found incompatibilities.

These problems are not a reason not to upgrade, but you should be aware of the possibility of them happening to you.

If the upgrade is a minor one, you may be able to use the older versions. We suggest calling the publisher to find out their policy on this. But the older versions could be used to expand your operations and introduce newer installations to the programs. If they were found to be worthwhile installations, you could then purchase the most recent version for them and place them on the upgrade path.

It may be that you do not wish to upgrade software at all. "If it ain't broken, don't fix it!" This is a noble sentiment. After all, you have spent hard hours learning programs yourself and helping other people as well. Why throw all this away for the sake of a dubious upgrade?

If this sentiment is true, we agree. But usually upgrades do not mean you must throw away all your hard-won knowledge. Upgrades build on knowledge you already have internalized. We've been "with" Microsoft Word since Version 1.0, through all major upgrades and all but one minor one. Things work a little differently now, but all things considered, the upgrades have increased productivity and ease of use. It has been worth it. Meanwhile, the commands have been memorized. We rarely need to look up anything.

Yet the pressure is still there. WordPerfect's latest release has made it, in our view, clearly the top word processor currently on the market. With the addition of imported graphics in WordPerfect, version 5.0, we actually considered switching. But, of course, Microsoft popped back with their own 5.0 that includes (you guessed it) imported graphics.

In any case, the publisher will eventually stop supporting older releases. Indeed, this is another impetus to upgrade. If they won't help you after a certain date, you don't have much choice.

In terms of configuration management, keeping all the versions straight is of major importance. That's why an inventory will be a dynamic program, rather than a static one. Writing down the serial number does not guarantee the job has been completed.

# 5 SOFTWARE POLICY

Microcomputers have not entered organizations through the front door. Instead, they have revolutionized organizations by using revolutionary tactics. Some MIS professionals feeling particularly besieged by all this insist the tactics have been those of guerilla warfare.

We would concede the point.

In our own organization, microcomputers initially appeared on manager's desks as personal purchases, not through any system-wide policy of procurement. As the machines became more and more indispensable a lobbying effort was introduced to get the organization to buy machines for the staff. Because budgets, manuals, and other products were all now produced by computer, the ultimate threat of taking the computer home became a real one.

The organization purchased the machines. But chaos was already planted. First, individual managers had developed personal preferences for software packages which they had purchased with their own funds. Since there existed no Big Brother to tell them what to purchase, they were very reluctant to change software, not to mention the brand of computer itself, though that was enforced by presenting each manager with a new machine.

There were obvious compatibility problems. Spreadsheets in use included Supercalc, Appleworks, and Lotus 1-2-3. Data base systems included Appleworks (again), R:Base, dBase, and First Choice. Word processors of choice included Volkswriter, Appleworks (again!), Microsoft Word, Zardax, and PC Write.

But another problem began to surface as each additional machine was added. In our view, organizations do not allocate sufficient resources to purchase adequate software for the machines. There is a tendency to concentrate on hardware costs at the expense of software.

When this happens, there is a strong pull to making copies of software to get the job done, just as employees originally brought in their own machines. The proliferation of such software is difficult to stop without Orwellian tactics of intrusion. But the fact is, copies of software, without a specific site license, are illegal.

This includes such basics as the disk operating system itself. Every machine in the place is supposed to have its own copy of DOS, with its own manuals no one ever reads and its own disks no one may ever use.

It doesn't really matter if twenty-five computers in the organization were loaded with the operating system from the same original disks; they have no serial numbers. But legally, each machine must have a purchased copy of the disks in order to run the system.

within the law. This adds about $100 to the price of any MS-DOS system, just like that.

The same is true of utilities such as Norton, Mace, and Spinrite. Yet the situation is confusing because licensing agreements aren't always very clear themselves. Many of them will say, "You can only use this program on one machine at a time."

This is a nice statement because it leaves open all sorts of loopholes. It doesn't say, for example, that you can't have the program *installed* on more than one machine. It says you can't *use* it on more than one machine at a time. For a utility program such as Norton, there are likely only a couple of people in the organization that can use the advanced diagnostics with any sense of competence. So why not load it everywhere, particularly if no one else even knows its there?

Because licenses don't always say that, because the law is very unclear, and because every software publisher has a different interpretation of what the licensing agreement means. This is particularly difficult because the words were originally used by some other publisher who interpreted them differently.

We suggest you err on the side of caution. The Software Policy listed below is the one in force at our organization. It is the official position of the organization. It says, in essence, that the organization intends to be legal about software; and that it expects all employees to comply with software licensing requirements. Employees are required to sign the document to indicate they have read and understood it.

Now follow the worst case scenario. An employee or group of employees has introduced the latest version of Norton Utilities into the organization, a program that has not been purchased. As employees find out how useful it is, copies are made and placed on more than one machine. It is cloned into other machines. Suddenly, there are a dozen copies floating around, all illegal.

Next in walks Peter Norton with the FBI and asks to see your machines. There's a court order. Apparently one honest employee found out about this little scheme and blew the whistle. Now you're in trouble.

The boss calls you, the Computer Guru, in to account for yourself. What do you do?

First, you can show your organization has a software policy designed to directly combat this problem. If employees have signed that policy and knowingly violate it, they can be dismissed.

Second, you can show through your inventory program a concerted effort to track software and to purchase packages in sufficient quantity to remain legal.

We suspect they'll let you out a little earlier for that.

## SOFTWARE POLICY

The software policy below was adopted by the Kitsap Regional Library Board of Trustees. Every staff member who works with computers is asked to read and keep a copy of the policy. A note to this effect is signed by the staff member and kept in the personnel file.

Kitsap Regional Library is increasingly taking advantage of microcomputers. Not only can they be used as terminals to our circulation system, they can also be used for word processing, budget management, and many other tasks appropriate to library operations. Software for these machines is also being purchased, most of which is not copy protected.

The Board recognizes the substantial investment software developers may make in providing products for use on these machines. The Board affirms that it intends to adhere strictly to Copyright regulations for software.

1. Any software normally used on a particular computer will be purchased for use only with that computer.

2. Software that is installed on a hard disk of a particular computer may not also be installed on another computer.

3. Employees may make copies of software for Library back-up purposes only. Copies for personal use are prohibited.

4. The Library will maintain a Central Registry of software and microcomputers which indicates which software package is assigned to which computers.

5. Back-up copies of protected software may be made by whatever means are necessary if guidelines above are followed, and all other provisions of the copyright holder's licensing provisions are met.

6. Employees who use microcomputers will be asked to sign the software policy document to indicate they have read and understand its contents. One copy will be placed in the employee's personnel file; a second copy will be kept by the employee.

Adopted by the Board of Trustees, January 20, 1988

## SPREADING THE LARGESSE

Updates may be one way to spread software dollars, particularly if the newest version does not radically alter the formatting or structure of the old program. When we converted from Microsoft Word 3.1 to Microsoft Word 4.0 we called up the company to ask their policy on such manipulations.

The answer, which we have documented, was that we could continue to use the 3.1 copies of the program, in addition to the newer version. Thus, we doubled the number of Microsoft Word copies we had available for our computers. When Ashton-Tate converted from dBase III+ to dBase IV, Egghead software advertised the program with the idea you could wind up with two copies by upgrading for $30 when dBase IV finally was shipped. In other words, it was a selling point that this could be done.

At first glance this seems like a chancy thing to do. We've been asking for some consistency throughout this work, then violated it as soon as we could get away with it. Indeed, we would guess some software publishers would take the stance that an upgrade does not entitle you to use both copies at all. You have upgraded a single copy to a newer version, but that means you still have only a single copy.

We plead poverty in this case and point out there really wasn't much difference between the old and new versions. Specifically, all the files produced by this word processor were totally interchangeable. It didn't matter which version you used.

Secondly, we confirmed the legal stance of Microsoft by talking to them and specifically asking the question if we could do this. We wrote down the conversation verbatim, got the name of the person we talked to, and filed the conversation away in a safe place.

Obviously, we now have two versions to track instead of one. We would suggest you not allow this to get out of hand so that you have three or even four versions of a software package. Sadly, this is entirely possible; versions are so often in changing. When Microsoft upgraded to 5.0, we paid our $5.50 upgrade fee, received all new documentation for all copies, and retired Version 3.1 permanently. We were then left with versions four and five, a happy circumstance since, once again, file structures had not changed. The macro language had, but most of our users do not use that portion of the program. Therefore, we were actually left with more copies of Microsoft Word than we had hard disks on which to install them.

This trick doesn't always work legally. It would be best to confirm with the publisher if there is some question. Lotus recently upgraded to Release 3.0 and 2.2. In this case the publisher specifically directed all upgrade recipient to destroy old copies of earlier versions. Obviously, they do not intend for your organization to double the number of copies simply because you upgraded.

There are also times when you may not wish to upgrade at all. We thought long and hard before upgrading to dBase IV, but ultimately decided to do it. The price was right; and we wound up with several legal copies for the price of one at retail. However, the new version was substantially larger (a whopping three megabytes compared to 500K) and slower than the previous version. Reports from the field of unresolved bugs and other incidents were also problematical.

# 6 SUPPORT

When computers sneak into an organization, the idea of support is a virtual oxymoron. The organization never agreed to have computers in the first place. Inevitably, the person who supports a growing stable of computers is the person most interested, the one who is termed the "guru" because he or she is six months ahead of everyone else in learning how to use the new machines.

At first the addition of one machine to the existing bunch may seem of no consequence. The guru has memorized what each machine does. He or she knows how many card slots are full, what size hard disk is on the machine, and what programs ought to be on the disk.

Through techniques used in this book and elsewhere it is possible for one person to manage a growing number of machines quite adequately.

At some point, however, PC management will become too much for one person to handle, particularly if he or she has other duties, which is, of course, inevitable. The key question to management is: How many PCs should one person expect to support? In other words, what is it going to cost us in staff time to have all these micros, really?

As might be expected, private industry has grappled with this problem and come up with some general guidelines. These are used in the formulas presented below.

Because micro support is often intertwined with larger system support, we have assumed terminal support is roughly equivalent to supporting a micro. Usually the people who run the "big" system have their hands in the micros as well.

The first formula seeks to measure the commitment of an organization to automation. A greater number of computers per employee would indicate a greater commitment. Most organizations should find their score is a fraction. After all, it is a rare employee who has more than one micro on his or her desk.

In this sense libraries may find themselves with higher scores than private industry. This is largely due to public access catalogs. Such a catalog can easily double the number of terminals in an organization without adding appreciably to the total FTE score.

We have presented the following formulas at several conferences and asked for feedback. We have also written about these formulas elsewhere. We apologize for repeating ourselves, but we really do wish to make a concerted effort to see whether these formulas will work.

Although we have several dozen written responses we do not yet have a sense of averages for libraries. Also, our first responses showed us that the initial formulas were much too complex. We have much simplified them here. After all, every complication increases variability exponentially.

If you care to take advantage of the free disk offer in the back of this book, we ask that you fill out a brief questionnaire to this effect. We shall publish results in the future.

## CPUs PER FTE

A "CPU" is a Central Processing Unit, just a fancy word for a computer, but more generic. A terminal is not always a computer per se, but it does function as a window to one somewhere. An "FTE" is a "full-time equivalent" employee. Two employees working twenty hours per week equal one FTE.

The library community has spent considerable energy defining how one ought to measure effective service. If you've ever perused *Output Measures for Public Libraries,* by Doug Zweizig, et al., you can see the results of that energy are quite extensive, even though they may be totally invalid (see Public Libraries, Fall, 1985, p.106). Some of the measurements are easy to make, and some require you to trip the patron on the way out to ask his or her sentiments on the effectiveness of the library.

We believe output measures are a good thing. We measure characters output to the screen, for example, to determine OPAC terminal use. We also use circulation output divided by the number of OPAC terminals to determine who gets the next one. The branch with the highest number wins a new terminal. We propose to add to output measures with the following new measure, CPUs per FTE, as well as second measurement for CPU support.

CPUs per FTE does not require restraining patrons; it is an easy measurement, requiring only simple mathematical calculations. You don't even need a spreadsheet! The idea of the measurement is to discern to just what degree a library takes advantage of computer technology. Whether this is a good thing or a bad thing is not for us to judge, being rather decidedly biased. But as with every other measurement, some definitions are necessary before effective use can be made of the measurement. The formula itself is fairly straight-forward:

CPU/FTE

**CPU:** CPU (Central Processing Unit) could be defined various ways. It's not quite as easy as it seems because it depends on your point of view. For humanoids, it could be the brain or the stomach, depending. Because our purposes are liberal and egalitarian, we define CPU as a computer or terminal, no matter how large or small. Thus a dumb terminal sitting on a front desk to handle circ transactions is a CPU because, we are sure, there is one in that box somewhere, if for no other reason than to control character generation on the screen. Also, Deep Thought has a single CPU (Yes, we know it has four, but really, that's more like left-brain/right-brain rather than separate brains altogether. A brontosaurus had a brain in it's tail, but that didn't help it survive the comet.)

For those who feel a big CPU should count more, we must point out that since each terminal counts as a CPU, it does garner extra points for itself. Therefore, a CPU can big or small, but it still counts as a single CPU. The more terminals it has, the more work it does. It gets credit, but not directly.

There is also no distinction between a dumb terminal and a full fledged micro able to leap tall buildings. We see no reason to award extra points for the fact that Lotus 1-2-3 is running on a manager's CPU compared to 3,000 books checked out on a dumb terminal at the circ desk. Which is more valuable? We don't know. Surely both make a contribution, so they both get counted. This means that a portable terminal gets a full count as well. All animals are equal in this scenario.

**FTE:** stands for Full-time-equivalent staff members, of course. Since this figure is well known in accounting and personnel circles, we needn't define the idea much further. Just take the number of hours worked by everyone at your institution and divide by the appropriate figure. If you're counting by months, for example, you should divide by the figure customary for your institution. This could be 160 hours, or 173.3, or whatever. Adjust for earned vacation if you like, as long as you are consistent.

The result might look like this:

| VARIABLE: | VALUE | SOURCE |
|---|---|---|
| CPUs: | 134.0 | Count them up |
| FTE: | 67.5 | Get from Personnel Dept. |

CPU EQUATION:

CPU/FTE
134.0/67.5
1.99

The CPU factor, then, is 1.99, nearly two CPUs per staff member. This measurement means little standing alone. In the example (which is fictitious), we consider it fairly high. Obviously, a library without automated services, public access micros, etc., would have a low CPU score. A library dedicated to such activities would tend to have a higher score.

## SUPPORT SERVICES

CPUs, of course, require support. Larger libraries, such as Tacoma Public, are hiring people to fill this role. Support includes technical support in fixing hardware-related problems, installation, etc.; and it also includes software support, usually in the form of user training. This is a cost that must be factored into the CPU score above. No special attention needs to be paid here, because the support technicians count as FTEs, regardless. At TPL, for example, there are 4 FTEs responsible for everything from LAN networks, the two minicomputers, including all operations, all the PCs, terminals, and modems, and all the software development, including writing the entire circ system.

*PC Week* (Vol 5:24, June 14, 1988) reports several interesting statistics along these lines. The larger the installed base of PCs, the greater percentage of time is spent managing them. The following figures break down the percentage of a PC technician's time supporting various functions. For sites with over 100 PCs, 26% of staff time was spent on hardware support, 10% on formal training, 7% on LAN management. These figures represent an increase in hardware support over a similar survey done in 1987, but a reduction in software training, at least on a formal basis.

Other activities include informal end-user training (23%), software development or customizing (15%), product evaluation and selection (12%), and what we interpret as reading *Byte* magazine (9%). Therefore we see that even in larger organizations, most training on use of computers is done on an informal (one-on-one instead of classroom) basis; and that trend appears to be increasing.

With Fortune 500 companies, the average number of terminals serviced by a single technician has risen to 77.5 (PC Week, Volume 5:23, June 7, 1988). This gives you an idea of the level of support required as you begin to implement more and more CPUs. For our purposes, we are still equating a terminal attached to a mini with a stand-alone PC. Many of the same sorts of things go wrong with each type. And for each hard disk on a PC requiring special attention, there is a phone line and multiplexer for the terminal with its own set of problems.

We propose, then, a second measurement of support, to include only the DP personnel compared, once again, to the number of CPUs installed on site. In this case, use the same sort of formula, but substitute the number of support personnel, in FTE, in place of the number of total personnel. The formula:

CPU + Printers / SFTE

CPUs: 134.0    Count them up
Printers: 5.0    Count them up, too
SFTE: 2.2    Number of support technicians assigned
M: 1.0    Maintenance Factor: See below

(5 + 134)/2.2
139/2.2
63.18

We've made a couple of changes to this second formula. The major one is that printers now count as a whole number. Printers are nefarious. They have lots of moving parts. They are subject to the worst dust imaginable. If they were human, they'd get black lung disease and be required to wear special clothing by OSHA. Their interfacing is problematical, at best. Printers all talk to their CPUs differently. Though sites often standardize on terminals (read: are forced to), they are likely to have as many different printer brands are as sold, probably more, since models change so often. It's only fair to count them.

Now, a problem. If you don't maintain the terminals, should you count them? Having a CPU with one hundred terminals attached looks great, but if they are maintained by your vendor, then you should hardly get to count them at their full percentage. Conversely, shouldn't a full-time computer operator who runs the mini, but never touches a terminal get more credit than for maintaining a single CPU, increased only because there is a printer and a couple of consoles in the computer room?

We suggest an adjustment that counts for something, at least. If you do nothing with terminals, then you still get some of the credit in the formula. If you do a lot, you get more credit. The actual adjustment we must leave to the individual site involved, but we do have a general guideline below. Argue if you wish. We'd be glad to make changes.

Often, maintenance by a vendor means you pay them, but you do most of the work. There are, of course, various degrees in between. We've been through every one of them as we moved from total dependence to total independence in this realm. It simply is not a black/white issue.

The first phase of this is that you pay the vendors one percent of the price of the terminal per month forever. When a terminal breaks, you call the vendor and tell them. The vendor fixes the terminal according to the schedule in your contract. Other than your involvement with the telephone, you do not mess with terminals. Score this situation a .4. Normally, we wouldn't give any credit at all, but this is where the factor of the mini computer operator comes into play. The larger the computer and more terminals involved, the more ".4" scores are attributed to the operator. Thus, some credit is awarded for this activity, the amount depending on the number of terminals, a rough measurement of the worth of the big computer.

Support personnel counts everyone involved in computer operations. We are factoring in time needed to run Deep Thought as well as handle hard disk complaints on PCs. This allows you to take into account those systems that are easy to run versus those which are more difficult. Ours is notoriously difficult to run, compared to a Dynix site, for example, which has the opposite reputation. In general, the bigger the computer, the harder it is to run anyway. But you get points based on terminals rather than difficulty or even size. If you have a CPU that requires three operators to run, but can only support ten terminals. then you are penalized appropriately. Your support factor will be way high.

The second tier is when you have a spare terminal provide by the vendor on site. A terminal breaks, and the vendor gets to fix it, but the vendor doesn't have time. Maintenance contracts for terminals are invariably weighted so there is no penalty unless they remain broken for two weeks. Besides, the terminal is at a remote branch. So you swap out the bad terminal yourself and haul the bad one in to a central site. The vendor then wanders in at his leisure to fix the terminal, which you then swap back out (if you're that silly) to the field again. Depending on how often you get roped into doing the vendor's work, score this .5 for occasionally to .8 for invariably.

The third tier is when you finally realize it costs more to maintain terminals than to buy them. So you fire the vendor and do it all yourself. You've reached the big time. Welcome and Good Luck. Score a factor of 1.0. If you deal with PC networking at all, we suggest factoring at 1.25. They are a pain, and you ought to get credit for the hassle.

If you have a mixture of terminals and PCs, some on maintenance, some not, then you'll have to factor each type separately. If you have some other combination of maintenance, then figure out a fair factor. Who says this is cast in concrete?

## Factoring Schedule:

| | |
|---|---|
| PC Networks, any type: | 1.25 |
| You do all the work, including repair | 1.0 |
| You swap out terminals and bring them in | |
| —always | 0.8 |
| —sometimes | 0.5 |
| You make the call, vendor does the work | 0.4 |

The resulting support score will not equate with the PC Week number at all, so don't be alarmed. They do not factor in doing backups on the mini as part of PC support. If the PC Week number were changed to include DP plant support, then we could compare. But it really doesn't have to equate with everything else.

Compare your resulting scores with other libraries, or with your own operation over time. You will have a relative measure of your standing for both degree of automation and the support process. At this point in the life of the formulas, we do not have a sense of what a given score means. That can come only after we have enough data to run some nifty standard deviation measures on the results. The point of this is that one should not be surprised at a conclusion that you need more help. The numbers above could help you quantify just where you stand. You might want to use them as justification for your next budget request, or hide them, depending.

If you have additions or corrections or different ideas about the justification for these measurements, we'd like to hear them. We'd be interested in your scores for this, of course.

# 7 HARDWARE

We are assuming one major fact in this book: You don't have much money. We know that. The idea is to stretch your purchasing dollar as far as possible. As public institutions, an increase in use does not imply an increase in funding. Consequently, productivity gains cannot be used in an expansion fueled by increased sales.

That means our institutions do not, as a rule, purchase high end equipment. There are few of the latest Compaq 386 machines, at ten thousand dollars apiece, in our offices. If IBMs are there, we have a special deal through the college or university that makes them competitive with other brands.

The other brands are all clones, i.e.: Computers that look like, act like, and run all software like the IBM true-blue, genuine machines. To understand the appearance of the MS-DOS clones requires a small amount of history detailing why things have turned out the way they have.

Clones are not significant players in the Macintosh market. Apple has managed to sew up the Mac hardware with patents and copyrights that make cloning the machine extremely difficult. Also, until recently the Mac has not had a significant enough market share to attract the massive investment it would take to clone a Mac.

As of this writing there are about three million Macintosh computers in the field compared to about 50 million MS-DOS machines. We're not claiming this makes MS-DOS machines better. Far from it. These are marketing facts you can check for yourself. There are more Chevies in America than Hondas, too, but *Consumer Reports* has different ideas about each manufacturer's reliability.

But look at what IBM did. Back when Apple was flopping over the Apple III, they actually sent a service bulletin to their dealers suggesting that if an Apple III failed to work, to pick it up six inches and drop it on the table. This became known as the "drop fix" which many of you may have tried with other brands. We certainly have. And after that Apple came out with the ill-fated Lisa, named after the illegitimate daughter of Apple's founder.

As all that was happening, IBM introduced the first substantial 16-bit machine to an 8-bit world. Then, fools that they were, they copied the original Apple II by implementing an open architecture. They published specifications, had five slots in the back for third-party add-in cards. Then they proceeded to invent newer and better versions of the same machine. First they came out with an XT, an IBM with a hard disk and 8 slots instead of five. Then they introduced the AT, a PC with a newer faster processor called the '286. In short, they copied the success of Apple, came in and took over the micro market. IBM acted very much like Apple was supposed to.

This was all accomplished by an IBM absolutely convinced that mainframes were the only real computers. But what they did was move one of their managers down to Florida with the charge to build a PC in just a few months. Phil Estridge was his name, and he took with him a few hot shot engineers who had purchased Apples for themselves. They operated as a small company under the umbrella of IBM. When they were finished, they had a wonderful machine. Compared side-by-side with the Apple II, the IBM was more robust, faster, sturdier, and capable of great expansion. It was built to succeed.

And it did with a vengeance. After the IBM juggernaut hit, helped along by Lotus 1-2-3 just as the Apple II had been helped by Visicalc, Apple was left with less than 20% of the market it had all but dominated. Of course, since the market was expanding rapidly, 20% allowed Apple to continue expanding as well. But as IBM was exulting over this successful venture, something else was happening:

The appearance of the clones.

Because of the open architecture of the IBM machines and the willingness of Microsoft to sell copies of MS-DOS to literally anyone who walked in the door, clones began appearing from every would-be computer manufacturer in the world. At first it was just a trickle. Texas Instruments brought out a machine that was just slightly different from IBM. Then Corona did the same thing. Neither were big hits. Then companies such as Leading Edge and Everex began to produce clones, many of which were imported. Compaq, the most famous, put an IBM in a lunch box so you could lug it around, at least for a block or so until your arm fell off, then followed with many more models. Mail order houses began to sell put-togethers. And the price of an MS-DOS machine went from several thousand dollars to several hundred. Suddenly, for the price of a good television set, you could buy a perfectly functional, 99.44% compatible 16-bit computer that could run any software that could run on an IBM.

Meanwhile, the Mac sold for extremely high prices and made inroads to the business market with desktop publishing and graphics applications. Now which computer was for the rest of us?

The numbers are staggering. 2.1 Million PCs were sold in stores in 1988, never mind the large mail order market. In comparison, Apple sold 270,000 Macintosh computers. But the really amazing part is within the MS-DOS market itself. Figures vary, depending on who is presenting them.

*PC Magazine* reports that of the MS-DOS machines in offices 28% were made by IBM. 72% were clones. Of the office machines, 54% are AT-class machines.

In other words, IBM is a large player in the MS-DOS market, but nevertheless a minority player. They don't run the show. By and large MS-DOS machines are clone machines. Many of them have no-name at all. The ones at our library are named after the Library. Of the 25 or so PCs in our Library, three are real IBMs; and that's only because we got them free through an LSCA grant. And now they're full of non-standard cards anyway. Only the motherboard and the case remain original IBM equipment.

IBM does make sturdy cases. We admit that readily. We are also quite convinced that some of the cases sold through mail order houses were cast in sand on a beach. They are made of a very cheap grade of metal which easily tears apart.

## SO WHICH CLONE?

There are several hundred companies which sell MS-DOS clones on the open market. Obviously, the management problem is how to get the most PCs per dollar and still ensure a machine that will work as advertised. 99.44% pure may be good enough for lots of applications, but what if your application is the one that won't quite work on the clone you choose?

Worse, what if you purchased a couple dozen of them?

**8088**

There is a second decision to make. There are currently three basic flavors of MS-DOS machine on the market. First, there are the oldest 8088 PCs. These have been on the market in one form or another since 1980.

Their advantages are declining, but they include the fact they are quite inexpensive at less than a thousand dollars. They will run most MS-DOS software; and they are quite adequate for many applications, particularly as dumb terminals hooked to a larger network.

Their major disadvantages are that they are extremely slow, and cannot support memory over 640K (though you can cheat), and will not run new software such as Lotus 1-2-3 Release 3.0, and Microsoft's Excel.

## '286

The second major flavor of MS-DOS is a 80286 (abbreviated to '286) machine, usually called an "AT." These machines run a much faster processor than a normal PC. They run from five to ten times faster. They can support expanded and extended memory; and they can run most software available today.

Typical '286 machines should retail for approximately $1200 to $2000. They are more expensive than the older PCs, but not that much more expensive.

If you have never used an AT for word processing, you cannot hope to understand how much faster they are than the vanilla variety. An AT running 10.0 on the Norton System Information test (SI) runs circles around the slower machine. The major visible change is the speed of screen updates. But speed also shows up in disk accesses, even though this is very much a function of the disk itself.

The speed issue is not just a speed-junky excuse to buy a more expensive machine. We're not limited to 55mph in computers. Speed becomes a critical issue as more and more programs require graphics and graphics interfaces. There is a lot more work for a computer to do to update a graphics screen at hundreds of dots per inch compared to a character-based machine that only has 2,000 or so characters to update.

## '386

However, many in the PC industry feel the 80286-based AT is "brain dead." They argue over whether Bill Gates of Microsoft said that fine phrase first, or whether it was coined by William Zachman of *PC Magazine*, or was it Bill Machrone? That doesn't matter, of course, but the idea expressed here is worth exploring.

The 80286 is essentially a very fast 8088 CPU. But it still has limited memory expansion capability and other technical limitations which make it awkward for developers to use.

A '386 machine can be purchased for $2500, but more typical prices are above $3,000. $5,000 is not at all uncommon.

The 80386 processor, however, eliminates these concerns. Machines based on the 386 are often still called ATs thus further confusing the issue, but the processor itself is the next generation up. On a scale of one to ten with the vanilla PC at 1.0 and a fairly fast AT at 10.0, the 386 machines run at 20 to 30. We have seen some as high as 50, though this is rare and expensive.

Speed, then, is an advantage to the newer machines. And with graphics coming on strong, speed is still an issue. The biggest advantage is that a 386 dispenses with any serious memory limitations. It is perfectly possible to cram as much memory into the 386 as you can afford. Some in the industry claim 16MB of memory will be standard in a few years.

The second major advantage of the 386 is its ability to run in so-called "protected" mode. This means it can behave as if it is several separate computers, all running different software packages. If there is a problem with one package that would cause a 286 machine to crash, it won't. The other software packages will continue running. Each one "thinks" it has the machine all to itself.

This is a major advantage in Windows-type environments where the computer is attempting to emulate the desktop. In a typical scenario, a user could be using Lotus in one window, dBase in another, telecommunications in a third, and word processing in a fourth. Each program would be running at all times. Flipping back and forth between programs would be done at the touch of a key. Trading data back and forth might take an additional couple of keystrokes, but it would still be easy.

The editorial stance taken by *PC Magazine* suggests that you should not buy a '286 machine at all. They maintain the '386 is the only machine to buy; and they have reduced editorial coverage of the older machines to back their stance.

The major argument for this move is that '286 users will lock themselves out of future advantages in software which will take full advantage of the more robust architecture of the '386 chip. '286 users will be left behind.

## '386SX

However, there is an alternative. It's called the '386SX. It is, in effect, a watered down version of the real 386. Technically, its data path has been reduced from 32 bits to 16 bits. It is also less expensive than its faster brother. Yet it will still address more memory and allow "protected mode" to operate. Currently we have one '386SX machine that runs at 18.0 on the Norton scale. Thus it is on the low end of the speed scale of '386 chips, but still nearly twice as fast as many '286 machines. Yet it will use all the cards from a '286, run all the software, and be the same to maintain.

Intel, makers of all these chips in question, has mounted a major frontal attack against the 286. They say the 386SX is the same price, so why use the 286 at all? Some market watchers claim the reason Intel is doing this is because they own all rights to the 386, but have given up second-sourcing the 286 to other chip manufacturers. If people do switch to the 386 *en masse,* Intel will benefit more.

Regardless of the reason, it is true that the 386SX is as inexpensive as the 286. Mail order prices for a complete 386SX are as low as $1300 from places like Zeos. These aren't cheaply made computers, either, but robust clones with good guarantees and excellent performance.

# TASKS AT HAND

No one likes to be locked out of future developments in the computing field. Yet we are still faced with the fact of no money. It may be that we cannot afford to stay at the head of the pack for computing, anymore than we can afford to change circulation system vendors every time someone adds new bells and whistles to an alternative system.

We believe a careful analysis of the tasks at hand is necessary before you can make an intelligent choice for the future. Also recognize that the machines you already have will likely not be thrown away any time soon. One thing we do in libraries is keep equipment until it doesn't work anymore. We have typewriters from the forties and furniture so old it qualifies as antique. Any business would have amortized such equipment decades ago.

Therefore you will have a mix of machines of differing capabilities. Fortunately, at least in the MS-DOS world, much of the software is backwards compatible. You can run Microsoft Word on an 8088, a '286, a '386, or a '386SX. You might not like it on an 8088, but it will run.

It is common to read industry accounts of someone lamenting another speed increase on the horizon.

"How fast do word processors have to go?" is the usual question.

**RECOMMENDATION**

In our view, the faster the better. It doesn't matter that you can type only so fast. That's not the point. When you start outlining, merging, paginating, and performing other advanced word processing functions, you'll appreciate the speed. On an 8088 based PC, you wait for the computer. On a '286 and faster, the computer waits for you. If you're using the PC for data base management or spreadsheet functions, the speed improvement is even more noticeable.

One of our programs, the Member Tender, is a list management program for libraries. We wrote the program using a data base system on an 8088 PC. Because of the slowness of indexing, we actually removed all real-time indexing functions to a separate step at the end of the data entry process.

With a '386 machine, this entire scheme could have been simply avoided. The '386 is so fast that all indexing could have been done "on the fly" without the user noticing any drop in speed.

This is a good example of how a faster machine allows programmers to address programming problems differently. In the first case, the programmer needed to work around the limitations of the machine to create a viable product. In the second, the machine was capable of taking on more processing tasks than were required.

Our entire approach in this book is to allow an organization to create a uniform interface without the necessity of resorting to GUI (Graphics User Interfaces) approaches and their attendant cost in overhead and computer resources.

Indeed, it is perfectly possible to use the entire suite of programs suggested here on a '286 PC which can be purchased for about $1300. If this approach meets your needs, we suggest you do it.

However, if you can purchase a 386SX for the same price, why not? It won't hurt you at all, and it might help. The point is that you ought to purchase machines for the task at hand, not for something which may or may not happen in the future. That changes too fast.

Since everyone in the business sells '286 and '386 machines, there remains the question of which one. One of the major attempts of this book is to actually suggest real things to you, not just get by with a statement that anything will do. That's what we detest to hear when attempting to sort out what to do.

## BUILD IT YOURSELF?

There are a couple of things not to do. One is to build your own machines. We have demonstrated several times how easy it is to build a computer from parts with your own Swiss Army knife. It is easy, we believe. However, it does not follow that we suggest you do this to equip an entire organization with PCs.

There is the issue of quality. Remember *Zen and the Art of Motorcycle Maintenance?* Robert Pirsig set forth on a journey to find himself. He was obsessed with idea of Quality; and this was well before Ford had thought of it. Recently we decided to test the bargain basement of quality by piecing together an IBM-clone. Parts had been building up for several years. There was an extra disk controller (with a serial port) in the drawer, and a CGA color card (with a parallel port) on top of the old filing cabinet. The color monitor was just sitting in a corner gathering dust. And we had that old 63 Watt power supply in a cardboard box somewhere. There was some extra RAM on an old Expando-card, too. That left need for a motherboard, keyboard, and a box to put them all in. These we purchased from Jameco Electronics. The box was $34.95; the motherboard was $89.00; and the keyboard was $59.95. So for less than $200 in outlay, we have another CPU, thus upping the CPU/FTE score around our house.

The box looks poorly made. Thin metal and cheap screws complete the unit which, if you force it, actually fits together just close enough so you can strip out the screws. It's one of those flip-top box affairs that opens up like a clam shell. We hesitate to measure for FCC emissions; just don't tell them. This has got to be a leaky PC.

The motherboard is unusually small, about the size of a piece of paper and not much thicker. The chips that weren't soldered in place were coming half out of their sockets. Some of the edge connectors look warped; and peripheral cards will not fit into them easily. In one case, we were forced to modify one of our cards by whittling away the plastic with a knife. The keyboard connector is placed off-center so that you take your chances plugging it in.

Same with the power supply. The older IBM unit fits in the space, sort of. There is no way to bolt the disk drive to the cabinet; and several screws with sharp edges poke out of the casing. The keyboard looks normal; and its switchable between PC and AT modes. Attention to detail is lacking, though. The "C" and "V" key caps were transposed. All these errors were cropping up until we compared that keyboard with an IBM and figured out why.

If we had purchased all the parts from Jameco, the price would have been $500, including their system discount. We would venture to guess this is about as cheap as you can build a PC today, from anywhere. You may be able to find a cheaper price if you investigate for a couple of hours, but that time will be more expensive to you than any additional savings off $499.

Still, you don't get much for this price. The PC will work, but barely. Add another drive for $69.00 or a hard disk for $250, plus some more memory for whatever it costs today. So, a functional machine with a hard disk still can be had for less than a thousand dollars.

And what do you get? A very, very cheap 8088 PC, which may last a long time. If it doesn't, you get to buy another one. If you like screwdrivers and are up for tinkering, this may be for you. However, we venture to guess you don't want to do that.

Secondly, you must be assured of compatibility. Buying parts from mail order houses does not do this. Thirdly, your time counts. It is expensive. It costs about $500 to put together a PC from parts, about $1100 for a '286. The happy fact is, they don't cost that much more to purchase fully assembled.

The value of the Swiss Army knife trick is to show how easy it is to maintain PCs, how you can install hard disk drives and change graphics controllers. But at a production level, it leaves a lot to be desired.

## MAIL ORDER BRIDES

We've been ordering from mail order houses for over ten years. Only once have we run into trouble with merchandise. Our card was charged, but the merchandise was not shipped. A call threatening FTC intervention brought quick results. Mail order companies cannot afford to make their customers that mad. The FTC aggressively pursues mail order fraud.

Mail order companies vary in their reputations and performance. Two which have proven reliable over the years are Dell Computer Corporation (800-426-5150) located in Texas. They offer reasonable prices and guarantees, including on-site service if you so desire. CompuAdd (800-666-1872) is another mail order house that has excellent prices as well as dozens of retail outlets all around the country.

For software we can highly recommend PC Connection (800-243-8088). Their prices are not always the cheapest, but they offer fast and intelligent service. The second software mail order firm we can recommend is Egghead Software, with branches throughout North America. This firm has a corporate accounts program that offers discounts in addition to their already low prices. Service is fast and efficient. Once you're set up with them, you need only call your account rep and say, "Gimme three Lotus and two Words." Everything else is automatic.

A disadvantage of many mail order companies can be that they do not take purchase orders. The ones listed above all do; and they have separate departments for their corporate customers.

## STATEWIDE AGREEMENTS

Public institutions can often take advantage of discounts offered through state purchasing authorities. Both Washington and Idaho, for example, have statewide master purchasing contracts with expedited delivery. That means that if you agree to purchase through the program, much red tape is eliminated. The computers available through the program have gone through evaluation tests to ensure both compatibility and reliability. Prices are discounted; and you can be assured of good service.

Why? Because the firm that lands such a contract for what can amount to thousands of PCs cannot afford to have so large a customer be dissatisfied.

Washington State currently has a contract for Zenith computers. Idaho, as of this writing, is negotiating a master contract.

## BRAND NAMES

We have had reliable service from two clone brands: Leading Edge and Club American. Both have proven themselves reliable over time; and both have handled every software package we've ever thrown at them, including some very esoteric software for terminal emulation, circulation system backup, and newspaper indexing.

Leading Edge ran into some trouble in 1988 when the American company distributing the computer went into involuntary bankruptcy. Today one of the wholesalers for the company has taken over distribution of this Korean clone, made by Daewoo Corporation.

Club Americans are often available through local suppliers, though not necessarily the established retail outlets in your area. We now have a dozen of these computers in service and have experienced no difficulties whatsoever.

Zenith Computers have been sold in droves to the government, including tens of thousands to the military. Zenith is also the preferred brand in the Washington State statewide master agreement. Though we have none in our own institution, continued reports from the field indicate Zenith is a reliable brand.

There are dozens of brands we have not mentioned here, including some such as IBM and Compaq, that are considered most reliable. However, these are expensive; and one of our guide words is "inexpensive." Absence of a listing does not imply a machine will not meet your needs. In summary, we can recommend Leading Edge, Zenith, and Club American without hesitation.

We have had some recent experience with two newer brands. These are Zeos and PC Brand, both mail order houses. We must give the edge to Zeos in this regard. We were most impressed with the finish and look of a 386SX we installed. We have had no trouble at all with this machine. It also comes with an excellent warranty, and price. The 386SX with a 30MB hard drive, 1MB RAM, and the usual condiments sells for $1619 complete. As with many brands, their advertised price of $1395 for the machine was only with 512K and without shipping. Still, a decent price for a good machine.

## LOCAL SUPPLIERS

Local suppliers can be an advantage when you're purchasing in quantity. We're not talking about the retail level at the local shopping mall, but the smaller outfits that may not even have a store front. If you can find someone in this category, you can get surprisingly good service.

Retail shops have been a disappointment for us; and there is a long-raging debate in the computer press about their natural role in the scheme of computerdom.

Retail sales people do not like discount shops at all. They claim people buy from the discounters, then expect service from the retailers. Yet the retailers have been cut out of the sale. Further, retailers must spend more for office space (mall spaces aren't cheap to rent). They service what they sell, hold the hands of purchasers, and they are available after the sale.

In our experience retail shops, even "name brand" shops, do not always offer the level of service they claim. We've had retail sales people tell us outrageous stories about equipment details that can only be chalked up to misinformation. At worst, we have more cynical explanations. Support has been nonexistent; and prices have been, well, full retail, for software packages we know better than the sales people at the store.

We must be fair here and say there are many sales people in retail computer establishments that are absolutely top notch in their knowledge and attitude toward service. We do not mean to cast aspersions at these fine people. Presumably, by your income, you know who you are.

The local suppliers we like to cultivate tend to be people who enjoy computers, know a lot about them, and are seeking to make a stab at supporting themselves through their hobby. As in any new business, these people tend to be under capitalized; and it is fair to say many of these businesses are shaky affairs, indeed.

But if you can find a knowledgeable person under these circumstances, they will go out of their way to cultivate you as a customer, a multi-unit customer at that.

In return, you can help them out.

For example, our Board of Trustees approves bills only once per month. Bills must be in the office the Friday before the third Wednesday of each month. We make sure a vendor's bill is in by that Friday, not the following Monday. Then the poor guy can get paid before 30 days are up, which is when most of his own bills are due. If we don't do that, we place the vendor in an awkward "cash flow" position, especially for a large order.

We also squeeze as much as possible in these situations. We expect no support from the local vendor. If you can relieve the local vendor of any hand holding at all, you might get a cheaper price. We still make these guys follow through on warranty claims, but we expect cardboard boxes at the loading dock. That's as much "service" as we want from them.

The accompanying graph shows what we think you should expect in the way of PC prices. If you're paying toward the top of the chart, you may want to shop around a little more. The lines represent the absolute lowest price we've verified for the type of computer listed. The high price can always travel into the ether. We've chosen to establish a bell-shaped curve to give you an idea of the ranges.

As you can see, the 8088 type MS-DOS machine is the cheapest. Expect to pay between $500 and $1200. At $500 you build it yourself from pieces. At $1200, you ought to get a hard disk and have the thing all set up out of the box. A good example of this would be a Leading Edge Model D. The 80286 machines range from $800 to $2000, with the same provisions. We have purchased several machines of this vintage in the $1500 range, including our Club Americans. The 80386 machines are still expensive; and here we've left the top end open. Go ahead: Pay $10,000 for one of these. You can do it. Make my day.

Figure 7-1 shows what has happened recently. The solid lines represent the traditional pricing curves for the three major types of machine. But the dotted line shows the effect of the 386SX. You can see that the introduction of this chip has changed the equation dramatically. Also, of course, the graph tends to migrate toward the cheaper end, thus squeezing 8088 machines until they are no longer viable.

## PRINTERS

We are quite convinced that for every computer model number in the world, there exist five printer model numbers, each a slight increment over the one previous. Printers are sold much in the

## FIGURE 7-1

Typical price curves for the various generations of MS-DOS computers. The 80386SX (dotted line) has pretty well killed sales of the 80286 variety computers.

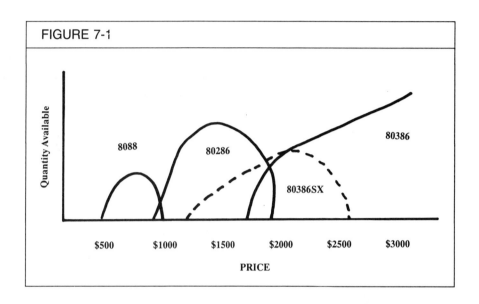

FIGURE 7-1

manner of model years for automobiles, except that printers change much more often. They all claim compatibility with "standards", of course, though sometimes that begs the question of just what standard really is.

Managing printers is easily as difficult as managing the PCs on which they run. They have lots of moving parts subject to malfunction. They eat paper at a prodigious rate; and ribbons are, in a word, problematical. If you've purchased your bevy of PCs incrementally, we guarantee each one has a different model printer. You were probably forced into it. In addition, you will likely replace the printer well before you replace the PC. Good luck.

For purposes of argument, we have identified four basic types of printer. They each may have their place, depending on circumstances. The four types are the "quiet" printer, the dot matrix, the daisy wheel, and the laser printer, each discussed below.

## 'QUIET' PRINTERS

There are two types of quiet printer, thermal and inkjet. Each uses roll paper especially adapted to this purpose. Both are reasonably quiet in that you do not hear the clatter of a daisy wheel nor the whine of a dot matrix overpowering all conversation. For areas such as a reference desk, they may be ideal, particularly if they are used for "quick" printing jobs, such as a screen dump of the reference PC. They aren't very fast, just quiet.

We use both thermal and ink jet varieties. After several years of dealing with both, we recommend ink jet printers, particularly those from Hewlett Packard. Why? They work, that's why. We have several "Think Jets" attached to Infotrac CD-ROM workstations. Other than needing to replace ink cartridges on a regular basis, these machines just keep working. We've replaced half the Infotrac PCs, all the CD-ROM drives more than once, and wanted to kick each contraption into submission like a recalcitrant Coke machine. But we have never sent back a printer, never had a serious problem with one.

Of course, having said that, we will undoubtedly pay for our crimes. Perhaps we have already paid our dues with the thermal printers. These are just as quiet, and they are much less expensive than the ink jets. But ours, at least, break so often that we have two for one PC. We are used to simply swapping them out when one breaks, to give us lead time to fix the old one.

The mechanism by which the print head moves is string, literally. The most common problem is an unraveled string. If you had hands the size of mice, then you could re-string the printer as fast as you could put in a new ribbon. Alas, that is not the case. We've also had problems with power supplies, broken bits of plastic, and heated print-heads that no longer work. Thermal printers are cheaper than ink jets, we admit, but if you must buy two per PC, it is hardly worth it.

## DAISY WHEEL PRINTERS

Daisy wheel printers come as close as possible to the IBM Selectric typewriter standard. For many years the Daisy Wheel defined the term "letter quality." The mechanism was a plastic petal where the letters of the alphabet were engraved. The wheel would turn just like a Selectric typing element, and strike the paper through a carbon ribbon. The result was a "typed" letter.

Daisy wheel printers are relatively slow. Where the average dot matrix printer screams along at 150 characters per second plus (cps), daisy wheel printers are lucky to reach beyond forty characters per second. One very expensive brand once bragged at fifty five cps, but that is as fast as we've ever heard for a daisy wheel.

Daisy wheel printers originally cost upwards of a thousand dollars. Slower ones were introduced a few years ago which cost about $500 and traveled at about 25 cps, but these were rare.

The reason they never caught on is that technology overtook them. The newer dot matrix printers began to re-define the word "letter quality" to mean dot-matrix print was acceptable. Dense "NLQ" (Near Letter Quality) modes on these printers came credibly close to producing fine-quality printing, certainly sufficient for correspondence. Some dot matrix printers also allowed carbon ribbons, further increasing the print quality. 24-pin print heads allowed finer shapes to letters. When speed was taken into consideration, only the purist demanded daisy wheel output.

From the other end of the spectrum came the laser printer. Though originally priced at several thousand dollars, the introduction of the Hewlett-Packard Laserjet II, a second generation machine, lowered the official price to $2695. But unofficial or "street" prices approached $1500. With perfect print-outs a reality, the expensive daisy wheel printer quickly became dead meat, the victim of a squeeze play from both ends of the printer market.

Today daisy wheel printers are used only where amortization is not in the vocabulary. We still have one clunking away in Administration, scheduled to be made into a coffee table later this year.

**DOT-MATRIX PRINTERS**

Dot-matrix printers are workhorse printers most of us know and love. There are many more models than can be detailed, now of two basic types. the first is the nine-pin variety, the second is the 24-pin variety.

The nine-pin dot matrix printers have been around a very long time. Epson Printer Company became a market leader early on by wrestling the entire market away from the thousand dollar Paper Tiger printers, on a permanent basis. It was quite awhile before anyone else made significant inroads in the marketplace; and meanwhile Epson became the standard.

The "standard" in this case refers to the computer codes used to generate certain types of characters. For example, to produce condensed print on an Epson, one must send an escape code, plus a numeric code to the printer. Once this is accomplished, the printer prints in condensed mode forming small characters which are equivalent to about 17 pitch (10 pitch is Pica, 12 pitch is Elite). This is "spreadsheet" print which allows you to cram about 135 characters onto an eight inch wide piece of paper.

The codes are "Escape" and "15". If you're working in Lotus 1-2-3, you must set up condensed print by typing "\027\015". Twenty-seven is the decimal equivalent to "Escape". If you want to switch from six lines per inch (yielding 66 lines per eleven inch page) to eight lines per inch, the Lotus codes are "\027\048". There are codes for emphasized print, double-strike print, italic print, etc. There are now literally hundreds of codes to what is called "Epson emulation."

We are willing to jump into a blanket statement and make the claim that all commercial software now supports the Epson standard. If you buy Microsoft Word, there is a driver for several varieties of Epson printers. If you buy WordPerfect or dBase or Paradox or any other package, they all have Epson drivers. To be fair, they also have drivers for other printers as well, it is true. But they *always* have Epson.

Therefore, any printer manufacturer which does not follow this standard is in serious trouble. They may think they have a better way of doing things, but they had better have true Epson compatibility somewhere along the line, or they won't sell any printers at all.

The problem is that everyone claims Epson compatibility here. Watch out! Some of them are almost compatible, but that isn't good enough. We have printers from NEC, HP, Epson, Okidata, Mannesmann Tally, Star, and others. They all have their problems, the Epson's because they are old and slow, and all the others because of Epson compatibility problems.

We'd like to standardize; and now we have quite a few Okidata 320 machines, which, if you get the *correct* Model 320, will emulate an Epson F86e, an older Epson that works just fine. If you don't get the *correct* Model 320, you're stuck with IBM Proprinter emulation, which is not as good a deal. IBM didn't define the standard this time.

We also caution you *not* to buy the latest model of a printer available. This is because the software companies lag behind in providing special printer drivers to fit the newest machines. We just bought Print Shop, for example, and tried to use it with an Epson LQ510, a recent update of the LQ500. No dice. It wouldn't work until we upgraded to The New Print Shop, which handled the new printer just fine. Our Okidata 320s are in the same category. Microsoft Word does not provide printer drivers for the newest model, therefore we use the trusty Epson FX emulation, which works just fine. As long as improvements are minor, we see no reason to jump on the latest unsupported bandwagon.

Another good reason to standardize is ribbons. They all take different ribbons, but if you can use the same ribbons on lots of printers, you stand to get a better discount and save serious money on puzzling out which printer ribbon works for which printer. We would guess that if you have a couple of dozen printers, all of the same variety, you'd save nearly the cost of a printer in ribbon costs and hassles just by buying only one kind.

Twenty-four pin dot matrix printers are an improvement on the nine-pin variety. Basically, they have a few more pins which can be placed in different areas of the dot grid (matrix) that makes up a letter. Combined with multiple passes of the print head, 24-pin printers can produce very well-shaped letters.

But there is a flip side to this equation. 24-pin printers have thinner pins. They're more fragile. Users are cautioned to be careful when using envelopes, card stock, mailing labels, or multi-part forms in 24-pin printers. They produce better print, it is true, but nine pin printers do credibly well these days and are sturdier.

The final decision must be based on use. We suggest that printers attached to online terminals or intended to produce massive print-outs be nine-pin printers. Those who use a printer mostly for correspondence might find the 24-pin printers more attractive.

In any case, we also suggest you should not spend over $500 for a dot matrix printer, $600 for a wide-carriage model which will print on fifteen inch paper. Dot matrix printers are excellent general purpose machines, but if you pay more for them, you are within striking distance of the laser printer price range.

## LASER PRINTERS

Laser printers are essentially copy machines hooked to computers. They combine the best of the three other types of printers. They are quiet like thermal and ink jet printers. They are faster than dot matrix printers. And their print quality is superb. With built-in character sets appropriate to most tasks, they are also capable of using cartridges or "downloadable" typefaces to turn them into typesetters.

Prices for laser printers have fallen drastically in the last few months. You can now purchase a Hewlett-Packard Laserjet IIP for less than a thousand dollars at mail order prices. Even the more robust Laserjet II is about $1500. At these prices, lasers have pushed daisy wheel printers aside and are even pushing seriously at high-end dot matrix printers. Lasers are a revolution in printing all their own, their host computers notwithstanding.

The Laser printers are the wave of the future, or even today. The IIP, noted above, has incredibly crisp print, the best a copy machine can offer. The IIP prints at four pages per minute, the II prints at 8 ppm. Four ppm is equivalent to about 300 cps, but this time the print is perfect. Plus, with a resolution of 300 dots per inch, these printers can be used for desktop typesetting very well indeed.

Laser printers retain their high quality because every time you replace a toner cartridge, you replace the entire guts of the machine, including the fragile selenium drum that can deteriorate with use. Thus, after about 3500 copies, you get to spend an additional $100-$150 for a new cartridge, but the cost per copy is still within copy machine limits.

It is possible to refill an old cartridge with new toner and pay less than half the cost of an entirely new package. However, remember that you will not replace the drum when you do this. Our laser gets about 3500 copies on a cartridge, with extensive desktop publishing use, which tends to use toner faster than typed copy. That is still well within copy machine price limits.

**Laser Standards:** There are two standards in this arena as well. There are Postscript laser printers, and those which emulate Hewlett-Packard's PCL, or Printer Control Language. Each has its advantages.

Postscript is a printer description language standard made popular by Adobe, Incorporated. The basic idea is to describe letters as mathematical equations, rather than a collection of dots. These equations can be manipulated depending on the size of the letter, but the same basic equations apply.

This holds true not only for size but also across machine boundaries. Thus a Postscript-based document can be transferred from a relatively cheap Postscript laser to a very expensive typesetter with no changes. Apple made Postscript popular by introducing the Laserwriter printer. The cheaper printer serves as a proofpress. High end lasers, by definition, are Postscript machines.

The other standard is Hewlett Packard, made popular by the Laserjet II, as well as its predecessors, and the new Laserjet IIP. These printers do not use Postscript, but instead rely on "bit-mapped" characters to be downloaded, a character at a time, from software based in the computer itself. Another possibility is for the bit-maps to be stored on cartridges which plug into these printers directly.

Either way, the bit-maps take a lot of space, either on a disk or in cartridges. In fact, a large bit-mapped character set, say sixty point Times Roman, can take over a megabyte of disk storage space. Unlike Postscript, you need a different bit-map for each size character. Thus you have one file for Times Roman sixty point, another for forty-eight, another for seventy-two, etc. This can add up to a tremendous amount of space.

Initially typefaces were sold with certain common point sizes. If you wanted different sizes, say Times Roman eleven point, which no one offers in standard packages, you had to buy them. But these days there are bit-map generators such as Fontware, sold by

Bitstream. These folks will sell you a typeface along with the Fontware. You can then "make" any size you wish. The resulting fonts are stored on the disk permanently.

This is a hybrid approach, really. On the one hand you can have any size you want, just like Postscript. But on the other hand, you wind up with bit-mapped fonts taking up a lot of space.

Postscript aficionados, especially those connected with desktop publishing or graphics, will tell you that is the only way to go. For their applications, it may be true, but the fact is, Postscript is expensive, slow, and heavily outnumbered by the Laserjets.

We maintain you can use a Laserjet II with desktop publishing as effectively as you can a more expensive Postscript printer. Further, if you really want Postscript on a Laserjet, you can plug in a cartridge and get it much less expensively than purchasing a printer designed with Postscript installed internally. If you are not interested in graphics or typesetting, then there is simply no reason for Postscript. A Laserjet with a cartridge or two will do you just fine.

But to the issue of standards, certainly never buy a laser printer that isn't either Postscript, if that is the route you follow, or Laserjet compatible. Laserjet compatibility is to laser printers what Epson compatibility is to dot matrix printers. There are no other choices.

**The IIP:** The most exciting Laser printer to come along lately is Hewlett-Packard's IIP. The "P" stands for personal. It is designed for lower use than the Laserjet II or IID (the double-sided version). It prints at four pages per minute compared to the Laserjet II's eight pages per minute, and the paper tray is much smaller. It holds about fifty sheets compared to two hundred with the II.

In other respects, the IIP emulates its big brother quite well. It has a cartridge slot, is capable of increased memory for downloadable fonts, and has actually more resident fonts that its predecessor.

The big advantage is cost, less than a thousand dollars at mail order prices. This brings the IIP into the range where you might consider them on a per-PC basis. Indeed, there are quite a few Local Area Networks which have been installed in the world for the major reason to share laser printers, which, until recently, have been very expensive.

But networks are expensive, too, even on a per-node basis. If each PC has its own dot matrix grunt printer anyway, the real cost of sharing a laser may be more than purchasing IIP printers for everyone.

# 8 LOVE IN THE TIME OF CD-ROM

CD-ROM may be a mystery to some of us, old hat to others, a rejected technology by yet others. In any event, there are many good and varied sources of information on the technical inner workings of this laser-optic storage and publishing medium. For that reason, I will simply make note of those sources when appropriate rather than provide yet another discourse on how the stuff really works (for those who just have to know each intimate detail). In the immortal words of L. Frank Baum, "Pay no attention to the man behind the curtain."

But to take full advantage of this exciting and powerful medium, we ought to know something about it: what it is, what it is not, how it differs from standard or traditional computer storage techniques, what it can be used for, and what problems exist in trying to incorporate it into the information technology strategy in our library today and in the future (as much as we dare predict).

## WHAT IS CD-ROM?

CD-ROM, an acronym for Compact Disc-Read Only Memory, is an electronic publishing and storage medium that relies on low-powered laser light to both imprint and read its contents. It is an offspring of the remarkably popular and trend-setting audio compact disc. In fact, many of this technology's short-comings, discussed in a moment, are a direct result of its similarity to its parent, the music CD.

Though we often find CD-ROM referred to as "an exciting new technological breakthrough", we should know that experiments with optical recording have been conducted for over 50 years, some with a fair degree of success. But, as is the fiendish and fickle nature of our capitalistic society, the "market" (that's us, folks) was thought not to be ripe nor ready for so whimsical a device. The most recent attempt at reaching the consumer market with optical storage "toys" was, of course, RCA's "Select-A-Vision" in the late 70s. Remember? Box office movies on a video platter; it looked like a phonograph record that you couldn't take out of its jacket. It quickly succumbed to the power and flexibility of videocassette tape, despite the fact that the videocassette industry itself was deeply embroiled in a "standards" mess—VHS versus BETA. In any event, laser beams were to remain the stuff of Star Wars or the weaponry in the daydreams of boys (and the Pentagon!).

It has been mentioned several times already that CD-ROM is a publishing medium and a storage medium. What does that mean? It is a publishing medium in that a master disc is made from which copies are pressed, literally, like the phonograph record pressing

**167**

process, or figuratively, like the printing process. The important thing to remember is that CD-ROM is heavily dependent on volume. It is not a cost/effective medium for small quantities. And, it is a storage medium, a quite remarkable one, with a capacity for storing over 600 million binary characters on one side of a single disc the size of a standard floppy diskette—which can store about a million binary characters on two sides (high density).

## WHAT IS IT NOT?

CD-ROM is not necessarily the best medium for holding dynamic information or data. As the rate at which data volatility increases, the utility of CD-ROM as the storage medium of choice decreases. The R-O-M part of the acronym means that the data can be read only—not altered, changed, or deleted (WYSIWYG—another infamous computer acronym for "What You See Is What You Get"). CD-ROM is not the consummate replacement for traditional storage media—fixed and flexible or movable disks, videotape, microform (fiche and film). CD-ROM has its place in the sun (don't take that literally please—discs *will* warp when left on the dashboard of the car), as discussed later, but so do other media. CD-ROM is not meant to supplant online database searching, but rather enhance it and make it more cost effective (also discussed later). CD-ROM suffers from slow access times—much slower than magnetic media. This is partly genetic—it is an offshoot of audio CD, a format in which rapid access was a detriment rather than necessity (we want to hear sounds and music at customary rates of speed). It is partly a result of the way information is encrypted on the disc itself—in an outwardly winding spiral, like a phono record in reverse, rather than in clustered sectors.

## WHAT IS IT GOOD FOR?

CD-ROM's premier benefit relates to its storage capacity. Being able to "buy" mainframe-sized databases exclusively for our own library is a significant change in our previous relationship with machine-readable information sources. Though we certainly shouldn't permanently sever our online connections with large informational databases, we can now luxuriously and autonomously "pre-search" for information, resorting to traditional on-line dial-up searching only for timely or esoteric information.

Compared to other forms of mass storage, CD-ROM has durability in its favor. In addition to being unaffected by magnetic fields (they're everywhere!), they are less sensitive to rough handling (within limits). But more importantly, they are not subject to wear and tear during their normal use because the mechanism in the player for reading the disc never comes in physical contact with the surface of the CD-ROM disc itself. Surface erosion ultimately takes its toll on virtually every other kind of storage media. The normal life expectancy of a CD-ROM disc is unknown! The only known enemy at this time is exposure to the atmosphere, where degradation through the process of oxidation of the construction materials is certainly possible.

CD-ROM may play a pivotal role in positively restructuring our organizational patterns as they relate to information storage and retrieval. Now, this is not exclusive to CD-ROM, but pertains to most all of data manipulation by computer. But CD-ROM may be significant in that it more closely affects individuals, be they library staff or library user, because of its association with the personal computer. Traditional schemes of organizing and storing information have been linear strategies—that means that both the information itself and the citation for it have been structured numerically and/or alphabetically. With no disrespect intended for Mr. Fulghum, the process of alphabetizing that we learned about in Kindergarten is an arbitrary system of organization, and is not all we need to know. Perhaps we should think about storing and retrieving information in a more "natural" way—you know, like we think or remember. The beauty of CD-ROM, and other computer-based retrieval systems, is that it allows non-linear search strategies to be used, like searching by keywords and combining (Boolean) operators. Weaning ourselves from alpha-based cataloging and indexing may be the most significant positive change in library organization since the Dewey Decimal System. CD-ROM, because of its relationship with the personal computer, may be just the tool to expedite that change.

## TELL ME HOW IT WORKS!

No. I refuse. It is a commonly held myth that it is only when we truly understand how something works that we can make the best use of it. Not so. How about nuclear fusion, for example. With apologies to those two scientists in Utah, we are all fairly competent users of a fusion reactor—yes, that's right, the sun—but a quick spot check around the neighborhood will show that very few of us really know how Ol' Sol works, eh? OK, I take some of it back. Cancer specialists are now revealing that some of us aren't such smart users of the sun. And look at the slow progress we are making with the implementation of photovoltaic power generation. But most of us get along pretty well with the sun, though I have seen people standing out in it on a hot day when there is perfectly acceptable shade close by. So, as far as CD-ROM is concerned, suffice it to say that it's all done with mirrors.

Well . . . Maybe just a quick explanation.

Just as the analog sound (music) for an audio compact disc is converted to a series or string of binary digits, so textual and graphic information—data—is converted to digital form so that it can be manipulated by a computer. For it is this marriage of microcomputer and CD-ROM that permits very large databases to be indexed and searched quickly in a non-linear (non-alphabetic) fashion. This machine-readable database is then reorganized ("pre-mastered") to match the program developed to ultimately retrieve the information it contains. A "master" copy, or mold, is made, generally of high-quality glass, from which the distribution copies are made, or pressed. The information to be encrypted has been translated into a series of microscopic pits which cause variations in the reflection of a lens and mirror-controlled (see, I told you) laser beam cast upon it by the playing device. The final product is the shiny mylar and aluminum disc that, again, is visually indistinguishable from the familiar audio CD. When placed in a CD-ROM player connected to a microcomputer, the disc reveals its contents on the computer screen in a manner dictated by the computer program developed specifically for that database.

If you want more technical detail, I suggest CD-ROM, *The New Papyrus: The Current and Future State of the Art,* and any of the CD-ROM related publications from Microsoft Press. In addition, there are several serial publications devoted in whole or in part to CD-ROM technology which usually contain "techy" information related to the "how" of it all.

## WHAT'S AVAILABLE ON CD-ROM FOR LIBRARIES?

Information resources currently available in the CD-ROM format generally fall into one of the following categories:

**Citation/Bibliographic Databases:** These may take the form of card catalogs, periodical indexes, directories, union catalogs, and MARC databases. Some are strictly utilitarian—that is, used for library cataloging and/or classification—while others are intended for use by the general public. Some are intended for both staff and patron use, providing reference and locative information. They generally provide little or no descriptive text beyond brief annotations.

**Textual Databases:** These may also take the form of indexes and catalogs, but also contain the full or condensed text of the reference. In addition, encyclopedias, almanacs, yearbooks, and other such textual reference works fall in this category. Entries may contain graphs, charts, illustrations, and photographs as well as text. Most allow for the capturing of the contents, either to a printer or machine-readable file.

**Specialty Databases:** These may contain special-purposes files for a number of different applications. Some may be collections of computer software programs. Others may be large collections of numeric data or formulae for engineering or scientific use. Most of these never see the printed page in and of themselves. Select portions of these databases are intended to be merged with other machine-readable data files in other computer-based applications.

Actual titles or products available are listed in a variety of sources. Try Meckler's CD-ROMs in Print, or various CD-ROM periodicals like CD-ROM Review or LaserDisk Professional. They contain comprehensive lists of products currently published in CD-ROM format.

Most CD-ROM products available today are merely replications or subsets of information resources that exist in another medium. In other words, the products represent another form of expression of information that is already available, though perhaps not with the same ease of access or economy of storage space. With that in mind, CD-ROM products should be evaluated with the following in mind:

- How does the price of the CD-ROM version compare with the product in its traditional release medium?
- Are the contents of both CD-ROM and traditional medium identical? If not, how do they differ? Is something missing? Is what's missing an enhancement or a shortcoming?
- Is access to the information contained in the CD-ROM product better, worse, or the same as in the traditional medium?
- Is the CD-ROM version easier or more difficult to use? What special skills are required, if any, to use the product?
- Can the information or data in the CD-ROM product be easily integrated with other software applications (word processing, spreadsheets, database management programs)?

- Is the CD-ROM product a *significant* improvement over what exists in our library now?

And most importantly,

- Is there justification for purchasing the CD-ROM product for our library? That is, is there truly a need that this product will satisfy which justifies its expense?

## WHAT EQUIPMENT DO I NEED TO USE CD-ROM?

As mentioned earlier, the power and utility of CD-ROM is a direct result of the marriage of laser-optic technology and microcomputer technology. The following components make up a CD-ROM "workstation":

- a personal or microcomputer. CD-ROM products are available for both Apple/Macintosh and MS-DOS-based computers. The majority of products that have relevance to libraries require the use of PC- or MS-DOS (operating system).
- at least one CD-ROM player. All CD-ROM products will require a player to read the data from the CD-ROM disc. Some products require more than one player because of the size of the information database. Most player manufacturers permit at least four players to be hooked or "daisy-chained" together. Major manufacturers are Amdek, Apple, Hitachi, JVC, NEC, Panasonic, Phillips, Reference Technology, Sanyo, Sony, and Toshiba. Many of these, and other electronics manufacturers, are beginning to produce clones to the three major interface configurations—Hitachi, Sony, and Phillips. Some models of players require a caddie for the disc before it can be placed in the player (Sony and Phillips mostly).
- an interface or connection to the computer. In order to attach the player(s) to the microcomputer, an interface card must be inserted in an empty expansion slot on the chassis of the computer. Yes, this means you must remove the cover of the computer and put your hands in there! A cable will then hook this card to the player itself, completing the connection. Additional cables will be required for multiple players, but usually up to four players may be run off that single interface card.
- a display screen or monitor. Depending on the requirements

of the program, special monitors and graphics adapters may be necessary to display graphic images, if, indeed, pictures or illustrations are part of the product contents. At the very least, a monochrome monitor will be needed to display information.

- a printer. Though it is rare to find a printer listed as an absolute requirement for operation, it is difficult to imagine exploiting one of these CD-ROM products fully without having one attached to the computer. An inexpensive 9-pin dot-matrix printer will easily suffice.

- configuration software. If microcomputer product marketing departments are sometimes guilty of a lack of candor concerning certain limitations or extra system requirements, then they certainly deserve the death penalty when it comes to special CD-ROM configuration requirements. In fact, it is misinformation, misunderstanding, or total lack of awareness on this topic that has led to the industry's worst nightmares in terms of the actual implementation of CD-ROM technology. The problems related to system configuration are of such a magnitude that the remainder of this chapter will be devoted to addressing that complex issue.

# CONFIGURATION CONSTERNATION

Many CD-ROM developers, in their enthusiasm and excitement to get their product to market, have overlooked a fundamental need or desire on the part of the end user—that of using their capital investment, i.e. the microcomputer, for a variety of tasks or chores. I'll borrow an old term from the U.S. Forest Service—the Multiple-Use Concept. That is to say, the microcomputer represents a resource, one that must be shared in most libraries primarily because of budget constraints, but also for reasons of economies of space and utility. Why, for example, would a person need to have two or three PC's on her/his desk when one, set up to switch between jobs would suffice? And, in the case of multiple CD-ROM product offerings in the library, why not simply dedicate a single PC and CD-ROM player (or two) as a CD-ROM Reference Workstation, running several CD-ROM applications from that one microcomputer. We encounter several problems:

1. Each CD-ROM product seems to have its own unique hardware requirements. Some require a hard disk to operate properly, while others will work with two floppy disk drives. Some programs require the full complement of RAM memory—640K—while others will work with 512K. Though primarily an option at this point, some take advantage of extended and/or expanded memory if available, with good performance characteristics relying almost exclusively on the ability to do so. Some CD-ROM products will run on most all major brands of CD-ROM players, while some are more specific about which players are supported by special "driver" programs within the retrieval software. Some products will run on either "IBM" architecture (what we know as the PC, and the new PS/2 family of computers), while others are more restrictive.

2. Each CD-ROM product seems to have its own unique file management and retrieval software, with its own special command to call up the program. Thus the user needs to somehow organize the programs' software—either manually, if floppy diskettes are used, or "electronically" through an operating system (DOS directories), if using a hard disk. Switching from one product to another is cumbersome, and it's quite easy for items to get misplaced, either manually or electronically.

3. Each CD-ROM product seems to have its own required configuration in DOS, and, in many cases, its own device driver. The MS-DOS operating system, needs to know certain things about the CD-ROM device being attached to it: how many memory "baskets" (buffers) are needed to hold the data it will be manipulating, how many file "handles" are needed for the program being executed, what the "name" of the peripheral CD-ROM device is, in some cases, and what special control instructions ("device drivers") are used with the specific kind of CD-ROM player being used. Even products using the same hardware usually require unique configuration settings and device drivers. These special tidbits of information can only be entered into the computer's memory at the time the computer is started up, necessitating a "reboot"

each time a different product is used. This is much too confusing and complicated.

As stated earlier, much of this relates to a myopic and egocentric attitude on the part of product developers. They fail to recognize that their product is probably not going to have sole and exclusive use of the PC that's used to run it. The hardware will most likely be shared by other applications, CD-ROM or conventional magnetic-based. A well-conceived CD-ROM application should acknowledge this, not frustrate it.

Let's look at what we can do about the problem that exists right now, hoping that current CD-ROM offerings will migrate to a standard configuration and that new offerings will take heed.

## HARDWARE

Choose hardware that is adequate to cover the most demanding requirements. Look carefully at what is already available in your library. For a PC workstation dedicated to CD-ROM applications, I suggest no less than an IBM PC/XT or compatible, with 640K RAM, a 20MB hard disk (the Seagate ST-225, or equivalent), DOS version 3.1 (or the latest DOS 3.3), a monochrome monitor with Hercules-compatible graphics capabilities, and a standard dot-matrix printer (80-column is usually sufficient). I've seen packages like this advertised for under $1500. Remember, however, that the PC/XT or compatible (basically, a PC using the Intel 8088 microprocessor) is not capable of expanding its useable internal (RAM) memory beyond 640K. If you intend to make a new purchase especially for a CD-ROM workstation, consider nothing less than an AT-style (Intel 80286 or equivalent) microcomputer. For a CD-ROM player, I suggest either the Sony or the Hitachi models. The most popular choice with libraries to date is the Hitachi 1503S. Cost of a single drive (either model) with controller card and cable is under $700.

## SOFTWARE

Use a menu approach for organizing and accessing the CD-ROM products you want to include in the reference workstation (see Figure 8-1, p. 184). Store the retrieval programs for these various products on the computer's hard disk, each in its own directory.

Create and use a collection of batch files to execute the directory changes and the program execution names. If you include the actual menu filename in its own batch file, you can then include that batch file name at the end of each program batch file to return you to the "Main Menu" when leaving any program. The use of a menu and batch files obviates the need for memorizing directory names and program start-up names. You simply select the reference source from the menu by selecting a letter or number corresponding to that product (the appropriate letter/number is actually the batch file name). This book has a section explaining how batch files are created and used.

## CONFIGURATION

A majority of CD-ROM publishers either mandate or allow their products to run in conjunction with Microsoft's CD-ROM Extensions, a software program from the developers of the IBM PC's operating system, which, in conjunction with your player's hardware device drivers, permits a large quantity of information to be accessed and retrieved from the discs themselves. This CD-ROM "extension" program overlooks, or "extends" the arbitrary 32 megabyte logical drive size limit imposed on the DOS operating system by the makers of DOS (yes, that's right—Microsoft). More on this later. You could theoretically install the Microsoft CD-ROM Extensions program when you first turn on your microcomputer, and it would remain there in memory, waiting patiently to serve any CD-ROM product that required it. And, in fact, you can do just that, using a statement in an automatically executed file (AUTOEXEC.BAT) to load it into the computer's random access memory (RAM) each time the computer is "booted up," or started. Each application could share this informational software, transparent to the user. The CD-ROM Extensions work in conjunction with instruction sets called "CD-ROM device drivers" to access and retrieve date from CD-ROM discs that have been encoded in either the so-called "High Sierra" or ISO 9660 data format.

As mentioned, many publishers have taken advantage of an enhancement to the Disk Operating System (DOS) supplied with the IBM PC/compatible microcomputer to overcome the maximum legal file size and logical drive size limit of 32 megabytes. Remember, we are dealing with a publishing medium that provides a storage capacity of over 600 megabytes. In order to use an MS-DOS compatible PC to access this information, the CD-ROM player and its disc must be treated like a giant hard disk without being hampered by storage size limit. Before this time, CD-ROM publishers had to work around this problem on their own, which led to serious inconsistencies. I am reminded of the video cassette "double standard"—VHS vs. BETA. In the Spring of 1986, a group of interested CD-ROM manufacturers met in Lake Tahoe to hammer out some kind of data encryption standard to preserve the industry from certain death due to this impending chaos. Those proposed standards, commonly referred to as the "High Sierra" standards, subsequently became the essence of the International Standards Organization's (ISO) 9660 Standard for recording CD-ROM data files. Version 1.0 of Microsoft's CD-ROM Extensions, released in the Fall of 1986, supports the High Sierra Standard, while version 2.0, released in the summer of 1988, supports the ISO 9660 data standard *and* the original High Sierra Standard.

In order to use the Microsoft CD-ROM Extensions, you need:

1. Version 3.10 (or higher) of DOS.
2. A device driver for the CD-ROM player to be used (usually supplied by the player manufacturer).
3. A CD-ROM product with data encrypted in the High Sierra or ISO 9660 Standard format.

The Extensions themselves really consist only of a single file, MSCDEX.EXE, running in conjunction with a device driver which is referenced in the statement "device = " in the DOS configuration file, CONFIG.SYS. A typical CONFIG.SYS file to be used with a CD-ROM application would look like this:

```
LASTDRIVE = Z
FILES = 20
BUFFERS = 20
DEVICE = hhitachi.sys /d:mscd000 /u:2
```

The first line, LASTDRIVE = Z, informs the computer that a peripheral drive, the CD-ROM player, will have to be accounted for in addition to those drives it can already identify. The statement only needs to indicate the largest drive letter to be used on the system, up to 26 (Z). A microcomputer with two floppy diskette drives (Drives A and B) and one hard drive (Drive C) would then assign Drive D to the CD-ROM player. If you were to attach two CD-ROM players, then the statement would read LASTDRIVE = E, since Drive E would represent the second player. By custom, assigning the letter Z as last drive surely takes care of any eventuality. The next two lines, FILES = and BUFFERS = , indicate how many file handles the program will need and how many buffers are needed to hold data, respectively. Be aware, however, that assigning files and buffers sets aside, or reserves, random access memory in the microcomputer, reducing the amount available for the intended application. Each additional buffer, for example, reduces the amount of memory available for an application by 528 bytes. Assigning BUFFERS = 20 means that the amount of available memory has been reduced by over 10K. A similar, but not so dramatic, reduction takes place in assigning the number of files that can be open concurrently. For each additional file above the default value of 8, available memory is reduced by 48 bytes. Assigning FILES = 20 (the maximum allowable) reduces the total available memory by 576 bytes. The last line is the infamous "device driver" line. Here, the computer is informed that a piece of hardware not necessarily recognized by DOS itself is going to be used. The instructions for utilizing it will be contained in the driver file—in this case, HHITACHI.SYS, a driver (instruction set) for the Hitachi CD-ROM player written by Meridian Data, Inc.. Optional parameters, or software switches, can follow the driver statement, the most important being the device name—here the statement /d:mscd000 translates "the device name for this particular driver is MSCD000." Note the device name delimiter (/d:). Actual device names are often chosen and set by the manufacturer of the device driver itself, and may be assigned as part of a program for "installing" the CD-ROM Extensions. If no device name is chosen, the Extensions will default to the name "MDIHSDVR." The option delimiter (/u:) is used to indicate the number of drives or units —in this case, we see that two players are attached. Unless specified with this parameter, one player is assumed.

When the computer is started, this file, CONFIG.SYS will be read, adjustments will be made to memory allocations, and the device driver mentioned in the statement DEVICE = will be sought for loading into memory. Be sure that the actual file, "HHITACHI.SYS" (or whichever device driver is chosen for the CD-ROM player used), is available in the root directory of your hard disk. An alternative is to detail the directory path as part of the device statement, e.g.: DEVICE = C:\SYSFILE\HHITACHI.SYS

The microcomputer then looks for a file named AUTOEXEC.BAT and executes any pertinent instructions contained in it. Here's an example for a typical CD-ROM/PC Reference Workstation:

```
CLS
ECHO OFF
DATE
TIME
```

```
MSCDEX.EXE /d:mscd000 /m:8
CLS
MENU
```

The lines CLS (clear screen), ECHO OFF (no DOS commands displayed) DATE (enter correct date) and TIME (enter correct time) are standard fare for an AUTOEXEC.BAT file. The next line beginning with MSCDEX.EXE instructs the computer to load the Microsoft CD-ROM Extensions into memory. Again, be sure the file MSCDEX.EXE is available, preferably in the root directory (if it is not, precede the statement with a pathname, i.e. C:\CDROM\MSCDEX.EXE...).

This now familiar Microsoft CD-ROM Extensions program will be referred to henceforth as MSCDEX. Verification of its successful implant in memory will be displayed on the screen. Notice the optional parameters following this filename. Again, "mscd000" (preceded by the delimiter /d:) is the device name for the hardware driver with which it will work its magic. The optional parameter, (/m:8), is used to determine how many sector buffers MSCDEX will allocate when it installs itself. The larger the value, the more sector cache entries will be made available and the less MSCDEX will have to read directly from the CD-ROM player. Increasing this value will steadily improve the perceived performance of some products up to the point that too much memory has been reserved. Remember, the application program needs room in memory, too. I've chosen a value of 8, which is conservative for initial memory of 640K, but probably about right for 512K (the default is 4). The determination of this value can also be affected by the number of players used, and depends entirely upon the application being run. If you want to fine-tune this value, experiment using the (/v) option switch. This parameter will display additional memory information during installation. You then can tell if you have exceeded the application memory requirements of any of the CD-ROM products to be used. Oh, yes, the last line, MENU, starts a batch file to call up a menu of CD-ROM applications to choose from.

Say, that's not so bad is it? So, what's the problem? Well, there are several.

**Problem One:** Not all CD-ROM products run under the Microsoft CD-ROM Extensions. This is not all bad. Some don't use the CD-ROM extensions, but it doesn't matter. They run fine without them, even if MSCDEX has been loaded into the computer's memory. An example is *BiblioFile*, from the Library Corporation.

Other products may not need the Extensions, but do need the valuable memory robbed by this program, and by the "files =" and "buffers =" requirements of the most demanding application (explained earlier). The CD-ROM Extensions from Microsoft belong to a class of software known as TSR programs (Terminate and Stay Resident) which operate in the background, transparent to the user, ready to be called up and used when needed. For example, loading the Hitachi device driver, the Microsoft CD-ROM Extensions, version 1.01, assigning 20 files and 20 buffers, and, of course, loading DOS (v. 3.1 in this case), leaves only 557K of free memory out of an initial 640K. Some CD-ROM products require a minimum of 580-600K of free memory, even though they may not require the Microsoft CD-ROM extensions. An example is an early release of the WilsonDisc retrieval software. It requires 580K of free memory, and will not run under this configuration, even though there is no direct conflict with the CD-ROM Extensions it does not need.

**Problem Two:** CD-ROM publishers still seem to have some special requirements, even though they may employ the CD-ROM Extensions from Microsoft. For example, some products may require more than one player, or may need a larger "files" or "buffers" requirement. Some installation instructions are quite adamant about this, indicating that the product won't run properly. For example, the McGraw-Hill *Science and Technical Reference Set on CD-ROM* (1st edition) requires that the file ANSI.SYS be referenced in the configuration file, along with FILES = 20 and BUFFERS = 20.

**Problem Three:** The "install" program that comes with most products may specify a device "name" that is not the same as the name specified in the initial loading of the configuration file and the CD-ROM Extensions. For example, the device "name" may have been specified as "MDIHSDVR" in the "device =" line of one configuration file and in the loading of the CD-ROM extensions, but is specified by another name in a batch or executable file portion of another CD-ROM application. Devices are called by specific names, and the name must be consistent for that particular device driver (you can use more than one device driver, but it must have its own unique name). Also, some "install" programs for certain CD-ROM products create, and more significantly, *overwrite* a configuration file (CONFIG.SYS) and/or an automatic start-up file (AUTOEXEC.BAT), destroying your initial configuration and auto loading, thus misdirecting the remaining CD-

ROM applications. An example is Bowker's, *Books in Print +*. It specifies and calls for device name of MSCD001, no matter what name you intended to use.

**Problem Four:** Some CD-ROM products require that the CD-ROM player be located on a particular drive letter. Although the computer can be informed of this with an optional parameter, it can only be told this once, at the time the CD-ROM Extensions are installed in memory. If two CD-ROM applications require that a different drive letter be specified, a conflict occurs. However, many CD-ROM products simply utilize the next available drive letter, no matter what that might be.

What can we do about this now? Aside from carefully choosing products that support a quasi-standard configuration (that is, a support of the Microsoft CD-ROM extensions and common manufacturers' device drivers), I offer these humble suggestions:

## FIRST HUMBLE SUGGESTION

It would be nice if we could adopt a configuration that satisfies the most demanding CD-ROM configuration. Examine the requirements listed in the installation section of each application's documentation. Since part of the problem involves reserving 11K of memory for files and buffers (FILES = 20, BUFFERS = 20), and many CD-ROM products will ask for that much, you're stuck here. The other big memory chunk is that reserved by MSCDEX (the Extensions), and the device driver (HHITACHI.SYS, ETC.). You may want to consider extended memory, if your PC hardware will support it. That is, break the 640K RAM barrier that is beginning to plague the installed base of original PCs. Microsoft's CD-ROM Extensions have an additional parameter, (/E), which allows MSCDEX to use extended or expanded memory if it is installed and available.

However, this is often not possible. An alternative is to resort to a concept of re-booting with a configuration and auto-start (CONFIG.SYS and AUTOEXEC.BAT) tailor-made for the troublesome application. This will necessitate re-booting with the new MSCDEX/device driver scheme when leaving those particular applications. Here's how to do it:

First, create a CONFIG file especially for the troublesome application. Name it CONFIG.XYZ, using a unique mnemonic extension for XYZ. The actual information contained in this CONFIG.XYZ file will come from the supporting documentation of the program of concern.

Next, create an AUTOEXEC file for this troublesome application. As before, give it the same unique mnemonic extension, i.e. AUTOEXEC.XYZ. We will use this AUTOEXEC file to start our troublesome application. But, within this file, we will also need to instruct the computer to restore our original "generic" AUTOEXEC.BAT file when exiting the program—that is, re-establish our "normal" configuration. We can do this fairly easily by making sure we have saved backup copies of our "normal" CONFIG.SYS and AUTOEXEC.BAT files under names protected from being overwritten. Use the DOS "copy" command to do so, like this:

At a DOS prompt, C, enter

```
COPY AUTOEXEC.BAT AUTOEXEC.NRM
COPY CONFIG.SYS CONFIG.NRM
```

Now AUTOEXEC.NRM and CONFIG.NRM reside in the root directory of our hard disk, and serve as backup copies of AUTOEXEC.BAT and CONFIG.SYS.

Now, let's create a batch file with which to start our "troublesome" program. We shall give the batch file the name associated with its menu listing. Assume for a minute that a hypothetical program, "SuperBase XYZ", is choice number 5 on our CD-ROM Workstation menu—that is, we are to press "5", then [ENTER] to start this program. Here is what the file 5.BAT might look like:

```
[1] ECHO OFF
[2] CLS
[3] ECHO ** PLACE SUPERBASE XYZ DISC IN CD DRIVE
[4] PAUSE
[5] COPY CONFIG.XYZ CONFIG.SYS
[6] COPY AUTOEXEC.XYZ AUTOEXEC.BAT
[7] REBOOT
```

The line numbers [N] are mine; they are not part of the batch file. Line [1] and [2] should be familiar to you. Line [3] prompts the user to insert the appropriate CD-ROM disc in the player or drive. Line [4] gives the user time to do so—the PAUSE command sends to the screen the famous message "Press any key to Continue." Line [5] copies our unique configuration over the original CONFIG.SYS file. DOS will look for a file named CONFIG.SYS and read its contents into memory when the computer first starts. Line [6] copies our unique auto-start instructions over the "normal" auto-start instructions in the original AUTOEXEC.BAT file. Line 7 causes the file REBOOT.COM, a simple public domain program that simulates the CTRL-ALT-DEL (or "warm boot") keystroke, to re-start the computer, forcing it to read this new and unique CONFIG.SYS and AUTOEXEC.BAT files.

This is what might be contained in the this AUTOEXEC.XYZ file, now the AUTOEXEC.BAT file:

```
[1] ECHO OFF
[2] CLS
[3] PATH=C:\;C:\DOS;C:\SBASEXYZ
[4] MSCDEX.EXE /D:XYZ001 /M:8 /U:3 /L:L
[5] CD\SBASEXYZ
[6] XYZ
[7] CD\
[8] NORM
```

Again, the line numbers are mine, and the first two lines are old hat by now. Line [3] is a DOS "path" command, which essentially says to the computer "Run any of the commands asked for. If you can't find them in the directory you are now working in, look in the following directories, in the following order." Line [4] loads the Microsoft CD-ROM extensions, using some of the optional parameters discussed earlier. Line [5] instructs the computer to change to the directory in which the mythical "SuperBase XYZ" program will run from. Line [6] issues the command to start the program, in this case "XYZ". Line [7] waits patiently until the application program is exited. This command instructs the computer to return to the root directory, where it will find and run a batch file called NORM.BAT (Line [8]). The batch file NORM.BAT, intended to restore our generic configuration used by most of our other CD-ROM applications, looks like this:

```
[1] ECHO OFF
[2] CLS
[3] COPY CONFIG.NRM CONFIG.SYS
[4] COPY AUTOEXEC.NRM AUTOEXEC.BAT
[5] REBOOT
```

Get the picture? This file is copying those backup copies of AUTOEXEC and CONFIG we made initially, restoring AUTO-EXEC.BAT and CONFIG.SYS to our normal configuration. Line [5], as before, runs the REBOOT program to force the computer to read these restored files, bringing us right back to our workstation menu. The whole point here is to make this re-configuration routine as transparent to the user as possible.

Since this alternative is much more cumbersome and time-consuming than using the approach outlined in the next section, use it only when the demands of the troublesome application leave you no other choice. I much prefer the next approach.

## SECOND HUMBLE SUGGESTION

I'll call this the "Lowest Common Denominator" approach. To compensate for the slight variations from program to program while still running under MSCDEX, select the parameters and requirements for the most demanding application as the ones to be used in creating this all-purpose, general configuration scheme. It may be helpful to create a "Configuration Comparison Chart" to make those choices, as in Figure 8-1. Include the CD-ROM products to be run along with specific configuration requirements, as described in the documentation for each of the applications.

The CONFIG.SYS file for this CD-ROM/PC Reference Workstation, based on the products selected from the chart in Figure 8-1 is as follows:

```
LASTDRIVE = Z
FILES = 20
BUFFERS = 20
DEVICE = ANSI.SYS
DEVICE = HHITACHI.SYS /D:MSCD000 /U:2
```

Note that the configuration for running WLN's "LaserCat" has a strong influence in this example, because that program requires

| FIGURE 8-1. CD-ROM CONFIGURATION COMPARISON CHART | | | | | |
|---|---|---|---|---|---|
| **Application** | **Device Name** | **Files** | **Buffers** | **#Drives** | **Dr. Letter** |
| Bookshelf | MDIHSDVR | 8 | 10 | 1 | next |
| McGraw-Hill Science Set | ANSI.SYS | 20 | 20 | 1 | next |
| LaserCat | MSCD000 | 20 | 10 | 2 | Drive L |
| PC-SIG Library | MDIHSDVR | 20 | 15 | 1 | next |
| Grolier | ANSI.SYS | 20 | 10 | 1 | next |
| Computer Library | any | 20 | 20 | 1 | Drive L |
| SilverPlatter ERIC | any | 20 | 20 | 1 | next |

two CD-ROM players, and the FILES= and BUFFERS= requirements are as demanding as most of the others. Note also the inclusion of a "call" for ANSI.SYS in the configuration; this is a requirement of some of the programs.

The DOS batch file, AUTOEXEC.BAT, used to automatically load the Microsoft CD-ROM Extensions, then bring the user to the main Workstation Menu could look like this:

```
ECHO OFF
CLS
DATE
TIME
MSCDEX.EXE /D:MSCD000 /L:L /M:8
CD\
CLS
MENU
```

The content of this batch file was described earlier. This is going to become our "Normal" configuration for purposes of returning our computer to its original start-up condition, as described in the first suggestion above. Therefore, make a copy of this file under the name AUTOEXEC.NRM. Notice the (/L:L) option switch in the MSCDEX line. It designates the drive letter "L" as the first available CD-ROM drive specification. Since the MSCDEX program is loaded at start-up time, you may want to edit those batch files that are a part of individual application programs which also contain a line calling for this file, MSCDEX.EXE. This avoids having the message "MSCDEX Already Loaded" appear on the screen. It does no harm, however, to try to re-install MSCDEX.

### THIRD HUMBLE SUGGESTION

You can edit any ASCII batch files or "install" programs that come with the CD-ROM applications that specify a device name other than the one you have chosen in your general CONFIG.SYS and AUTOEXEC.BAT files. Use DOS's "EDLIN", any text editor, Sidekick, or a word processor like WordPerfect or MS Word which allows you to import and export text files.

As in the example cited of *Books in Print* +, simply find the line in the batch file that loads the program, change the device name from "MSCD001" to "MSCD000" to fit the example above, then save the file under its original filename. As for instances in which the "install" program attempts to create or write over configuration and auto-start files, make a back-up of both your CONFIG.SYS and AUTOEXEC.BAT files. You could copy them right there in the root directory, giving the copies names like CONFIG.NRM and AUTOEXEC.NRM (shorthand for "NORMAL"), for example. This would be a good idea in general. Then, if there has been some alteration, or you employ the strategy for "rebooting" described in the previous section, you can simply copy these back-up files over the altered ones, restoring your original configuration. Again, make sure you have taken care of any misdirection in the application's batch files, especially in the naming of devices.

### FOURTH HUMBLE SUGGESTION

The naming of specific drive letters becomes a difficult problem to solve only if references to drive letters are hard-coded in the application program itself. Most CD-ROM programs are "trained" to go to the next available drive letter, regardless of letter designation. For instance, the documentation for the *PC-SIG Library on CD-ROM* (April 88 issue), instructs the user to switch to Drive D on a hard disk system (C for dual floppy systems). If, as in the example above, the most demanding program requires that the program start at Drive L, we simply go to Drive L to use the PC-SIG Library disc by typing L: at the C> prompt. References in batch files to a particular drive designation, like D, can be edited to reflect this change as well. The "menu" batch file to choose this application can also direct the retrieval software to the appropriate drive.

# Conclusion

There pervades in this "industry" an attitude I shall call, for lack of a more appropriate term, vendor "CD-centricity," defined as "the tendency to assume that my CD-ROM product is the only one to be run on this PC." It is not, and cannot be so. For many libraries, dedicating a PC and CD-ROM player to each CD-ROM application is out of the question. Though prices, thankfully, are dropping for both PCs and CD-ROM players, hardware still represents a very significant investment for the majority of libraries. Those CD-ROM publishers and vendors that adhere to standard hardware drivers and support non-specific extension parameters—in other words, make an effort to allow use of their products without making special modifications to the microcomputer's configuration each time they are run—should be eagerly sought out and supported. The decision to purchase products from those that do not should be carefully considered.

# TOOLS AND SUPPLIES

By now you know PC Management entails more than simply filling out purchase orders. It is a "hands-on" job that requires no small amount of aggressive learning on your part. It's not all software loading, either, even though we've detailed a software tool kit elsewhere that you'll probably find very handy.

There is a hardware side to all this; and it involves tools. Tools are like drugs; they're addictive. The first one's cheap, even free; and it's usually a screwdriver, perhaps liberated from the janitor or the AV Department. ("I'll bring it right back, I promise!") Of course, if they made all connectors with thumb screws, you wouldn't need a screwdriver, at least not as soon. Alas, most DB connectors have those impossibly small screws which never fit into those little holes around back of the CPU or the terminal or the PC or wherever.

We maintain you'll be buying tools for a long time to come. If you can equip yourself in advance with a few of the tools your likely to need, life will be easier for you. Below is our assessment of what you will need to manage a stable of PCs. You'll probably be able to get by at first with only that liberated screwdriver, as long as you carry it around with you everywhere. We've been through many a computer crisis armed with only a cheap plastic screwdriver. Sometimes lugging around an expensive cache of tools only serves to complicate the issue.

The neatest screwdrivers are called "jewelers screwdrivers." They're made solely of metal and they have a twirly handle. You bury the twirly end in your palm and twist the screwdriver itself while the twirly thing stays still. They are easy to control and come in all those tiny sizes computer makers seem wont to use. You can also get them with hexagonal blades. They can be purchased two ways: One is with a single handle and a set of blades which screw into the base itself. The other way is a separate driver for every size. The cheap sets costs about ten dollars; more expensive ones go from $35 up to $100.

Of course, once you have a jeweler's screwdriver set, you won't want to share, so you'll have to break down and give the set back to AV and get one of your own. After awhile you'll need more screwdrivers: a phillips in several sizes, standard, nut drivers, and maybe a Torx-head driver for those special jobs. Before you know it, you'll have a drawer full of screwdrivers. If you can keep them away from the janitor and the AV department, you'll be able to unscrew any connection made.

If you're always dealing with standard parts, connecting only printers to PCs, then consider yourself very lucky. In our institution, PCs are used as terminals hooked to the Mini-Computer,

Deep Thought, as often as they are used as stand-alone computers. As a result, we must create our own cabling to hook up to the mini. They don't make these things off the shelf. If you are working with a Local Area Network, we suspect you'll be doing a fair amount of wire twiddling as well.

That means another set of tools including needle-nose pliers and wire cutters, strippers, and a crimp tool or two or three, depending on what you need to crimp. If you're into coax or cable (Goodbye printers; hello LANs), you get an entire parallel set of tools to set along side the first. They're from a different branch of the evolutionary tool tree. Nothing fits both.

If you're lucky, some people will give you tools. IAC, the makers of Infotrac, for example, send a small flat-blade screwdriver and a hex key with every new Infotrac set-up. When they come in for the first time, we trade the tools for installation. We promise to install the system if they let us keep the tools. We were greedy at first, but now the place is over run with stubby screwdrivers and a bunch of hex keys, all the same size.

As you can see, it's easy for this to get way out of hand. One should not grovel for tools, should one? Of course not. So the only way to handle this addiction is to feed it. Give in. Buy tools. Buy as many as you can get away with. Buy more than you need. You'll find a use for them, we promise, even if you just wind up loaning them to the AV Department.

We were lucky. A few years ago we decided to maintain our own terminals. We discovered the vendor of our mini computer was charging us, on a monthly basis, the price of a new terminal to maintain old ones. When we first purchased the system, the field engineers thought it was really neat every time they came over because they got to ride a real ferry boat to get here. In the Summer when the sun and the mountains are out at the same time, it's really pretty; and they liked it. They got to sit down for an hour and cruise over the blue water between all the islands, drooling over all the waterfront property. But then a couple of other libraries bought the same system; and coming over to see Deep Thought became a drag. The Field Engineers began to develop the attitude of commuters tied to a damned ferry schedule; and they really didn't want to see us anymore. Besides, so-and-so's disk just crashed.

Anyway, since we were fixing all the sticky keys and running around to all the branches, we decided we could do terminal maintenance ourselves. So we bought a *big* tool kit with the maintenance fee for the first month; and then we bought a bunch of new terminals with the rest of the money we saved. It's been two years; and now we have lots of tools and lots more terminals than we had before. Like I said, it's lucky we bought the tools.

As part of this windfall we began purchasing more and more PCs as well. Of course, all the tools fit PCs just as well as they did terminals. In fact, there's not much difference between them. Terminals are a little less complicated, but they're pretty stupid as well.

The easiest way to get set up in this process is to buy a complete tool set from a recognized supplier. You *could* buy one of those dippy tool sets they sell in the Inmac catalog, but we humbly suggest these tool sets provide more profit to Inmac than they do useful tools to you. A comparison study we performed on the offerings of sets from Inmac compared to tool distributors revealed that you get many more tools per dollar if you are willing to shop around. One tool broker you may want to investigate is *Jensen Tools,* 7815 South 46th Street, Phoenix, AZ 85044. (602) 968-6231. These folks have a wonderful free catalog full of everything from the King Kong Tool Kit to the Bomb Squad Kit. In between are many different tool kits designed for telecommunications, field engineering, and many sub-specialties. They usually have several options for case design and contents. Price examples include $675.00 for the Bomb Squad kit; $300 for the Supervisor's Kit; and $250 for the basic field engineer's kit. Other kits range from a low of about $100. The Bomb Squad is just about the most expensive kit you'll see advertised, unless you fill a cheaper kit with lots of diagnostic tools that drive the price higher.

A characteristic of many of these kits is the large supply of sample items. If you've never used solder wick, for example, they'll throw in a small roll so you can see how it works. They hope to get you addicted, of course, and they are a ready supplier.

For PC maintenance we suggest purchasing a good case to go with a modest kit. A deep case provides a sturdy, lockable compartment for all the tools; and also allows for expansion when you decide the tools in the Bomb Squad Kit aren't quite sufficient to meet your expanding needs. Many of the cases come with foam rubber inserts which can be cut to fit the tools you decide to carry around.

Another characteristic of the Jensen tools is that they are top quality. These screwdrivers aren't from those K-Mart blue-light specials where you get twenty wooden-handled screwdrivers for $7.77. These are real tools with, in this case, a lifetime guarantee. That means if one breaks, you get another one free.

This is a critical point. You can spend less money on cheaper tools. Cheap tools break and require replacement. The tips break, sockets burst, and handles fall off. Then you get to replace them. If you replace them with more cheap tools, then over time you have a set of cheap tools requiring replacement. If you buy the more expensive tools, then you will always have them. Your biggest problem will be how to hide them from the janitor.

Another point. Tools are an ongoing cost not because they will always break, but because there will always be new diagnostic tools you will require. We are pretty well fixed for basic tools. One hammer, barring abuse, will last a long time. But there always seems to be a new diagnostic tool that would be nice to have and would make life easier. If not a digital multi-meter, then a new crimp tool or soldering iron, or maybe a line voltage analyzer so we could prove it's the power and not our terminals that are causing the problems.

## TOOL LIST

This tool list is meant to be general. It includes a lot of the tools we have and which have been proven useful over time; and it also includes a few things we don't have but know we could use effectively. Obviously, your situation is different. If you do not maintain all your terminals and PCs, run your own wire, and otherwise tinker, then perhaps you can get by with less. But this still isn't a list of tools required to take apart the mainframe (well, it could come apart with these; it just wouldn't go back together.)

**PC Tool Kit (Basic):** Figure about $100 for an extremely basic kit. *Moore Business Supplies* (P.O. Box 5000, Vernon Hills, IL 60061: 800-323-6230) sells a "Mini-Computer Tool Kit" for $79.95 (75F77891). The "mini" refers to the kit, not the computer. For many of us, this kit will be satisfactory for most basic operations.

**PC Tool Kit (Advanced):** Figure $500 for an intermediate tool kit that will get you through most any endeavor. Jensen sells a computer systems maintenance kit for $409.00 (G-76RL: 65 pieces). *Specialized Products* (2117 West Walnut Lane, Irving, Texas 75038 (800) 527-5018) sells a similar kit for $515.00 (SPC 55AL: 47 pieces). These kits contain all the screwdrivers, nut drivers, pliers, wrenches, and similar tools. If you buy one of these kits, you shouldn't have to worry if you have the right hex driver or a mirror to see around a difficult edge. Just to keep things in perspective, Inmac sells a Field Engineer's Tool Kit (#7434: 54 pieces) for $499.00. Often the type of case can add or subtract a full hundred dollars from the price of a kit, therefore a strict comparison based on the type and size of screwdrivers is not always a fruitful approach.

**Multimeter (Voltmeter):** A multimeter measures voltage or continuity. You can get a true multimeter from Radio Shack for about thirty dollars. These really do have multiple gauges on the front. The gauge you read depends on what setting you have on the machine. Newer varieties use digital displays (LEDs or the more common LCDs) to display information. A Voltmeter can display AC or DC Voltage. AC is in the range of 120 Volts, useful for determining whether a socket really does have electricity. DC voltage is in the range of 5 to 12 volts, useful for measuring power output on the small side of power supplies to see if circuit boards really are receiving proper voltage. Many voltmeters also have a setting to test continuity. It's either one of these or the old flashlight and battery trick. We suggest a substantial but not fancy Voltmeter. We have a Fluke Model 73, which lists for $79.00 in the *Specialized Products* catalog. You can pay a few hundred dollars for one of these if you want to, but if you do not need the advanced functions, it's not worth the extra money. You'll have to put in an hour or so learning to use one of these instruments, but once your confident with one, the information gleaned from its use can be invaluable.

**Crimp Tools:** It depends on what you're crimping, of course. LAN Managers will need an entire set of coax crimp tools. Those of us who use DB-25 or DB-9 connectors found most often on PCs need an entirely different set. If you're into RJ-11 or RJ-45 crimping, you need a different set still. The most common crimp tool is sold by many mail order supply houses for about $45.00. It is basically a pair of pliers with funny ends that crimp the small gold-plated insertion pins of many different sizes. Inmac sells one of these for $39.95.

We find the basic crimp tool adequate, but barely. If this is all you have, you'll have to learn patience to use it properly. If you have a problem with dexterity, these things can be well nigh impossible. If you do a lot of crimping, you may want to investigate a more expensive tool. *Black Box* (P.O. Box 12800, Pittsburgh, PA 15241 (412) 746-5500) sells a crimp tool for insertion-type pins for a whopping $116.50 (Part #GG-FT070). This thing crimps only two sizes of insertion pin (24 gauge and 28 gauge), but it provides the best crimp we've ever seen. The pin fits into the tool only one way. You then crimp down slightly before inserting the wire, which will only go so far into the tool. You then crimp all the way; and the tool will not let go until you've pressed far enough to attach the pin permanently to the wire. With an audible click, the tool lets go enough to remove the pin and wire. Once you get the hang of this tool, you'll get a perfect crimp every time. It may sound expensive. But for us, it was worth it.

**Break-Out-Box:** In its most primitive form, a break-out-box (BOB) simply splits out the leads of a cable into separate connections. The idea is to plug the end of one cable into one side of the BOB and the end of another cable into the other side. The connections are thus "broken out" into connection points on the box which are much easier to manipulate than the cable connections themselves. You connect the two cables by attaching small scraps of wire (jumpers or "leads") from one connection to its opposite side. Only the cables that you connect actually have continuity and will pass signals.

Why would you want to do this? One common example is when hooking up terminals to a host, or external modems to a PC. With the common RS-232C interface standard, specific pins are assigned specific signals. Thus, pin 2 is always transmitted data, and pin 3 is always received data on a DB-25 or DB-9 connection. To further complicate matters, there are two types of devices: DTE and DCE. DTE stands for Data Terminal Equipment, such as a terminal. DCE stands for Data Communications Equipment, such as a modem. Now, if you are connecting a piece of DTE equipment to a piece of DCE equipment, you can use a cable that has all pins connected straight-through: Pin 2 to pin 2 and pin 3 to pin 3. This is because the equipment itself is wired to accommodate this. It knows that data sent out on pin 2 must be *received* on pin 3. Therefore, the connection itself is wired internally to accommodate this. But if you connect two of the same kind of devices to each other, pins 2 and 3 must be "swapped" so that data out on 2 come in on pin 3 on the opposite device.

AH! But it's still worse. Some equipment is switch selectable. All you do is flip a little dip switch on the equipment (A series of these cursed little switches is called a "mouse piano"). With the switch flipped DCE becomes DTE and that all means the cable must be different.

Some modems commonly connected to PCs have a software selectable switch of this type. These software switches do allow versatility and more choices, but it is terribly difficult when you need to hook up the device correctly in order to access the software switch to see what the setting is. We've been in several Catch-22 situations with modems set like this. About the only thing you can do is proceed through an orderly trial and error process in hopes of hitting on the correct setting.

The point really is that you don't know starting out what you're dealing with. The exact same connection between a modem and an IBM PC which works won't work between the same modem and a PC clone. What's the likely cause? Pins 2 and 3 need to be swapped. How do you find out? Use a BOB before you tear into the cable. That way you can flip the leads on the break out box to see if anything changes. It's a lot easier than destroying a cable to see what they've done to you this time. Then when you do make up a cable, you'll be sure it will work.

The example is easy. But BOB boxes can be used for every lead on a standard cable. Not only that, the more advanced boxes can send current over conductors to test continuity. If voltage is sent over pin 4 and the little LEDs on pins 5, 6, 8, and 20 all light up, what have you found out? That someone has wired these four pins common inside the cable itself. Rather than tear into the cable, the Break-Out-Box lets you know how everything is wired.

The BOB can be cheap or expensive. With Voltmeters we advocate staying on the cheap end of the scale. If you really need a more expensive one, then you know more than we do about them anyway. But with a BOB, it may pay to spend a little more at the outset. Everyone sells them. Inmac sells a cheapie for $45, but the only guarantee is that it will break. We broke a similar one we purchased from Black Box with no apparent effort. The leads are cheap and the connections, once split apart, do not retain their resiliency. Connections are made entirely manually.

On a more expensive BOB connections can be made with mouse piano switches. In fact, many have a switch that automatically flips lines 2 and 3, since that is probably the most oft-encountered problem fixable by one of these devices. In addition, more expensive boxes have LEDs that light up when a signal is present. Some even have tri-state LEDs that glow a different color, depending on which direction a signal is traveling. All these also come with manual jumpers and double-duty gender bender cables that allow you to hook any sex cable to the box. Expect to pay between $100 and $300 for an adequate device. Take a look at the Inmac catalog to get an idea of the different types available. The other supply catalogs also sell these devices, but the descriptions are better in Inmac.

**Insert/Extract Kit:** This set of tools allows you to insert integrated circuits into circuit cards, or pull them out. Because there are so many different sizes, several tools are needed to accommodate any given task. You can't pull out a memory chip with the same tool used for an EPROM chip. Quite often a board manufacturer will send a cheap extraction tool with a card. For example, Microsoft includes an extraction tool with their Mach 20 speed up boards. This allows you to remove the CPU and replace it with a cable that runs to the 80286 on the card. We have a collection of these cheapies collected over several years.

Unfortunately, they're quite cheap. And though they will extract well enough, they surely won't insert; and insertion is where you will run into problems. Jensen, once again, sells such a kit for $47.00. For your money you get five tools that, if you use them, are worth it. You'll be able to deal with anything from an 8088 CPU to those tiny 4164 RAM chips that seem to go bad all at the wrong time. The tools are a must for stuffing RAM boards, but even if you do no RAM stuffing, you may find them useful.

We have found that many times we can fix a flaky terminal or PC by taking off the cover and removing the socketed ROM chips on the motherboard. We remove them, and then plug them right back in again. This clears up the problem. It doesn't always work, but it works often enough that we have adopted this as a normal maintenance procedure.

Surely the tools listed here aren't all you need. If you run a lot of cable, for example, you'll find a few other tools useful, too. Meanwhile, the tools listed above will give you a sound basis from which to build a better collection.

## SUPPLIES

Supplies and suppliers are often given short shrift by vendors of computer systems, large or small. A simple statement of "Plan for supplies" is often the only clue that supplies for computers and computer equipment will be a big part of your life. This is unfortunate because supplies are an ongoing cost, the amount of which is not trivial at all. Whether your site needs printer ribbons which cost $5.00 apiece or a voltage protector at $200, the fact is that you will keep buying these items, over and over again, year after year, for the life of the system.

For example, anyone who claims computers reduce the need for paper is crazy in the extreme. Computers generate more useless print-outs on wide green-bar paper than any other piece of equipment except a printing press itself. To speak of paper in reams of 500 sheets each will no longer be an expression of sufficient magnitude. Computers force one to speak of paper in terms of boxes of 5,000 sheets each. In large installations, paper is discussed on a per-pallet basis.

But that's not all. The word "supply" casts a wide net to include many accessories now sold for the sake of data processing. Furniture of all types, sound shields for printers, and large reels of cable are just a few. There are surge protectors to purchase, disk boxes to consider, and all manner of storage systems for all the supplies that will now be accommodated.

Where do you get all this stuff? Not surprisingly, many vendors have jumped into this marketplace in an attempt to satisfy even the most demanding data processing professional. Before long, you will be on the mailing list for several dozen catalogs. You will receive phone calls from boiler room operators intent on sending you a free fishing rod in exchange for the purchase of cleaning equipment and inflated prices. You will be courted with full-color advertisements, cold-call salespeople, and all manner of good deals if only you will purchase in quantity.

## THE VENDORS

Pricing alone can be deceiving. Indeed, as any trip to a Baskin and Robbins ice cream parlor will testify, the suppliers may have particular reasons to charge different prices. Their overhead may be more as they purchase a wider variety of goods in order to meet their customer's needs. Even warehouse space is not cheap.

Shipping may be very deceptive as additional charges are added that may make what seemed to be cheap prices into mediocre prices, or even prices which are most expensive.

Speed of delivery is not the least important item. In a speedy data processing environment, a needed item is usually needed yesterday. If Inmac or another supplier can guarantee delivery at a premium price, no one may care. Indeed, even shopping for bargains takes staff time. Wading through two dozen catalogs may not be money well spent if you know anything you like can be found in two or three proven suppliers.

A Returns policy may also make a vendor stand out. Inmac, not known for low prices, will take nearly anything back no questions asked, even if its your goof. Other vendors have been known to place the words "nonreturnable" right on the invoice.

Billing procedures are also important, particularly to institutions trapped into a long payment cycle. Some vendors will automatically extend credit and await a check patiently. Others want a long application form; or they'll call on day 31 demanding to know if you understand what "Net 30" means.

Incidentally, if ordering information contains a statement such as "2% 10/Net 30" this means that if you can pay them within ten days, you can deduct 2% off the price charged. This may not seem like much, but add up the price for supplies for a year and see if this savings does not amount to more than is suspected. In any large institution, Accounts Payable is a different department. You likely will not have much say in the matter.

A minor difference is an 800 number. They don't come cheap; and their use represents a considerable investment. Most suppliers have them. If they also have them available during normal business hours in your time zone and on weekends, they may be a more attractive supplier.

The range of a supplier can also be important. An East Coast supplier will probably not be the best choice for a West Coast installation unless there are mitigating factors. Freight charges alone would tend to make them non-competitive. Several suppliers on this list have regional warehouses which can cut down shipping costs and provide products faster.

The final potential difference is qualitative and subjective. How does the normal sales person treat you as a customer? We were recently short-shipped even though a supplier claimed everything was in the box. We called to complain. No questions. The sales person immediately sent out the remainder of the order. That means we will probably buy from them again. They owned up to their mistake and earned our patronage. Simple.

Below is a thumbnail sketch of each of the suppliers on the sample list. Included is address information and other pertinent details.

**American Computer Supply, 2828 Forest Lane, Dallas, Texas 75234. 1-800-527-0832.**

64-page quarterly catalog. No minimum listed. Shipping is $3.00 minimum, cheapest way. 7:30am - 6:00pm Central Time. 90 day satisfaction guarantee. Free gift incentives. 30 day open account. Offer to research special needs.

American is a middle-range supplier and not inexpensive. In our surveys they frequently were the most expensive supplier or near the top.

**Avnet Direct, 10000 West 76th Street, Eden Prairie, MN 55344. 1-800-877-2226.**

96-page catalog. No minimum listed. Shipping free on prepaid, otherwise added. 30 day satisfaction guarantee. Several offices nationwide. Open accounts are net 20.

Midwest supplier catering to micro and mini users. They are a little weak on cable parts, but they sell terminals, CD-ROM drives, and printers through the catalog, unusual for a supply vendor. Pricing is middle road, never cheapest.

**Thomas Discount Computer Supplies, 5633 W. Howard Street, Chicago, IL 60648. 1-800-621-3906.**

64-page catalog. $30.00 minimum. shipping added. Prices are mid-range. We found their catalog a little skimpy on information about ordering and policies.

**Richard Young Products, 508 S. Military Trail, Deerfield Beach, FL 33442. 1-800-325-0136**

A very fancy catalog, 88 pages. It looks like they have co-op advertising with some of their vendors. Minimum is $50.00, and orders less than $100 get charged an extra $5.00. Net 10 (!) with approved credit. Special statement to the effect public institutions are on terms, which we take to mean they won't wait 30 days for payment for those of us stuck in long payment cycles. Their guarantee is a little weak: 30 days, plus 15% restocking fee if there is no defect. Contrast this to Inmac, for example, which will take anything back, no questions, for 45 days.

However, Richard Young prices are very good, especially in quantity. They're worth a look just to compare. They frequently compare top quality, name-brand items. In our surveys they frequently turned up as cheapest supplier.

**Dartek Computer Supply Corporation, 421 Eisenhower Lane South, Lombard, IL 60148. 1-800-323-1872.**

60-page quarterly catalog, complete with free gifts for reaching a given dollar amount. Minimum order is $25.00. References required for open account. Free shipping on pre-paid orders, UPS surface, others available. 8:30 - 5:30 Central Time. Guaranteed satisfaction or your money back, 45 day window. Midwest location.

Dartek is middle of the road on pricing and came out cheapest for FX-80 ribbons, but you must purchase at least six. They were also cheapest on the crimp tool, by a dollar. They are reasonably comprehensive and have all but the BASF tape on the sample list. They do carry an assortment of common PC software at some discount off retail. They also have some hardware such as hard drives and printers for microcomputers.

**Devoke Co. 1500 Martin Ave. Box 58051, Santa Clara, CA 95052, 1-800-822-3132.**

96-page catalog. Minimum order $15.00. Call 6:00 am - 5:00 pm Pacific Time. Merchandise is FOB Santa Clara, so you pay shipping. Normal is UPS Surface. Others available. Guaranteed satisfaction with 45 day window. West Coast location.

Devoke claims several products as exclusive, though often they are just variations on a theme. Their PC floor system stand, for example, is available many places and is only superficially different. Nevertheless, there appear to be several at least rare products. The Menu-Master and Menu-Finder products, for example, allow thumb-sketch guides to be placed on or near a CRT screen. These "reminder" sheets can help with training in software use in a site which has many terminals all running the same applications.

Devoke's pricing tends to be on the high side, and the fact that you pay freight will raise the price even higher. They still charge $29.50 for a box of Maxell disks, well above average. There are lots of cables and rack-mount switches, but few tools or other products oriented specifically to the large user.

**The Drawing Board. Greenwoods Industrial Park, P.O. Box 2995, Hartford, CT 06104, 1-800-243-3207.**

135-page quarterly catalog, The Drawing Board has a "frequent buyer club" which earns you discount points for products, vacations, etc. No minimum order. Automatic $500 credit line. $1.95 handling charge no matter what. Free shipping on prepaid orders, otherwise shipping is added. Satisfaction guaranteed for one year. Eight strategic locations nationwide. 24-hour shipping.

The Drawing Board once supplied a very small catalog. Over the last year they have dramatically increased in size. They are not the cheapest vendor, but they have a lot going for them. One of their strong points is FORMS. They have forms for accounting and payroll programs for many different vendors. They will also custom design form-feed stationery, forms, or labels for you. They also have a very good selection of ribbons. They are not strong on tools or cabling, but the wide variety of stationery makes up for it.

**Global Computer Supplies, 2318 East Del Amo Blvd., Compton, CA 90220. 1-800-8GLOBAL.**

92-page catalog, monthly. No minimum order. References required to open account. Shipping is added to all orders. No hours listed. Guaranteed satisfaction, 30 day window. Three locations: NY, GA, CA. 24 hour shipping.

Global is a strong contender for best supplier, though perhaps a little too bureaucratic in opening accounts and customer numbers. They consistently scored cheapest in our market basket survey, with only one exception. They also have a number of products not found elsewhere. They sell toner cartridges for laser printers and a strong selection of surge suppression devices. Global also sells our favorite DB-25 hood with a built in strain relief, a device they have patented. Their catalog features a separate section on "new" items, a welcome relief for a catalog which appears monthly. Their weakness is a lack of paper products, though they do have a few stock forms. Many of their products sporting the "Global" label are in fact products manufactured by other suppliers.

In one recent incident, we called them to place an order for hoods. All sales representatives were busy, so they took our number to call back, but they never did. Strange behavior, no conclusions.

**Inmac, 2465 Augustine Drive, Santa Clara, CA 95054. 1-800-547-5444.**

Latest catalog was 194 pages. No minimum listed. Automatic $200 credit. Shipping is added to orders. No call time restrictions. Special 'address goof' phone number 1-800-826-8180. Guaranteed satisfaction, 45-day window. UPS surface is normal, but others available. Most orders shipped same day as receipt.

No one who has been automated long can escape an Inmac catalog. They have several, including an Introductory, a "Biggie," and a special "Clear Signal" catalog for telecommunications, and one specifically designed for personal computer users.

Inmac is everywhere; and they try to live up to a speedy reputation. Of you need it now, they will accommodate you. But you pay. Inmac isn't cheap. They don't claim to be. But they have made progress and are no longer as outrageously expensive as they used to be. They also have a "new products" section, which for these folks is essential. It would take a day to give attention to the entire listing of products. It's difficult to say what they are strong in because they have everything.

But we do have a couple of concerns. The Inmac guarantee of quality is sometimes necessary. We have obtained products in the past which are not of the highest quality, but if you complain, they will take the products back. They are also somewhat inflexible. If it isn't in the catalog as listed, it is unlikely it can be ordered. Inmac doesn't sell DB-25 connectors by themselves, for example, though they will sell a kit. Of course, this may also be true of other vendors as well.

Our opinion is that if you need something in a hurry and either don't or can't care about price, order from Inmac. If you have the time and inclination, shop around first.

**Misco, One Misco Plaza, Holmdel, NY 07733. 1-800-631-3500.**

132-page catalog, quarterly. $25.00 minimum. Quick Credit, but not automatic. Shipping is added to orders, UPS surface normal, others available. 8:00 am-8:00 pm Eastern Time. Two warehouses: NJ and CA. Guaranteed satisfaction, 30 day window. Same day delivery for orders received before 3:30.

Misco is a large supplier, nearly as large as Inmac. They had all but one item on the market-basket list and the "cheapest" price on floppy disks. They were frequently second-cheapest on other items. They have a good selection of tools and analyzers; and they claim exclusive products. However, just as with other suppliers, their Misco-brand products extend to the silk screening on the product only. Plotter pens, for example, are exactly the same as the pens sold by Inmac under their own name.

We judge Misco to be a strong all-around supplier which has a good selection. It is not overwhelming in any one area. Their policy of Net 20 is more restrictive than most other suppliers who ask for Net 30, but they probably won't refuse your business if you are a few days late.

They will sell component pieces of DB connectors in small quantities. You aren't required to purchase an entire kit just to get a connector.

**Moore Computer Supplies, P.O. Box 20, Wheeling, IL 60090. 1-800-323-6230.**

72-page catalog, quarterly. No minimum listed. Credit after due consideration. Shipping charges (and sales tax) added. Call 8:00 am - 5:00 pm all zones, 7 to 7 Eastern. Guaranteed satisfaction, 30 day window. In-stock guarantee or 10% off next order. Several warehouses nationwide. Next day emergency service available. Free gift incentives.

Moore is part of a large paper-products company. As such it is particularly strong on forms, including custom imprinting, which they will ship within 6 working days. Moore is lacking in tools and cabling parts. We judge their pricing to be not competitive. They did not win "cheapest" in any of our market-basket products.

**Uarco, 121 North Ninth Street, P.O. Box 948, DeKalb, IL 60115. 1-800-435-0713.**

72 page catalog, quarterly. $25.00 minimum. Shipping is added. Call 7:30-6:00 Central Time. Guaranteed satisfaction, 90 day window, gift incentives. UPS surface, normal, overnight available.

Uarco is nationwide with 13 distribution centers, a number of plants, and a large number of sales offices. Their 90 day guarantee is the longest of any of the vendors surveyed. Their prices, however, tend to be on the high side. They won none of the "cheapest" awards in our market basket. As an example, an insertion tool which cost $2.80 from Source, not noted for cheap prices themselves, cost $5.95 from Uarco. Uarco does have their own forms factory and can provide customization to your needs.

## LOCAL SUPPLIERS

Local suppliers are not likely to have large catalogs mailed nation-wide. And they can be cheaper than the larger outfits. A good place to look for a local supplier is the telephone book, particularly under paper products. Our local supplier, Western Paper out of Seattle, is the cheapest source of bulk paper we have yet identified. They offer free shipping. In fact, the day after an order a large semi pulls in front of the building with all the supplies ordered. It is very fast and personal.

Local suppliers are also very competitive. It would pay to shop around and pit them against one another for the best price and service. But be sure it is apples and apples that are being compared. What may look like a higher price from a supplier who delivers to your door may in fact be lower when the price of shipping is added to the lower-priced competitor. The weight of paper products is not insignificant.

Local suppliers may also offer the advantage of personalized service. Once you have established a rapport with the local sales rep, he or she may be trained to take care of you. The good ones will be able to scope out your own operation and know when you are running low on paper or tapes. Their "cold calls" rarely are, proven when you call them as they walk through the door.

Local suppliers may also offer to store supplies for you free of charge. This may allow you to obtain a larger discount by ordering more than you normally have room to store at your own site. It's good business for the supplier, too, of course.

Certainly local suppliers are not to be overlooked. They should be first on the list when you attempt to set up a supply network to support your DP organization.

## COOPERATIVE PURCHASES

If you run a DP shop which is part of a governmental agency of any sort, check into inter-governmental purchasing agreements. In Washington State, for example, all the junior taxing districts such as libraries, fire districts, and even local water districts, are eligible for "State Contract" pricing.

For a nominal yearly fee, all these agencies can take advantage of large volume discounts available through the clout of the State. In addition, Washington has a "Central Stores" facility also available to all agencies, complete with their own door-to-door delivery service. Prices for commodity items are sometimes as little as one third of the retail price for the item.

School districts may also have banded together to obtain volume discounts in the same manner. This may be true not only for supplies, but for larger pieces of equipment as well. Apple Computer Company has always been fond of allowing "educator's discounts." Mini-computer suppliers will also take advantage of a promised large volume by allowing generous discounts as well.

## SPECIALIZED SUPPLIERS

Most of the suppliers listed so far are general suppliers which have a wide variety of items. Some with roots in the paper industry have concentrated on forms and paper products at the expense of cabling and tools. Still, the products sold by one supplier differ very little from those sold by another.

There are a few specialty suppliers which have a peculiar market niche. One of these, for example, is:

**Texwipe Computer Cleaning Products, 650 E. Crescent Ave., P.O. Box 308, Upper Saddle River, NJ. 07458. (201) 327-5577.**

It is tempting to make fun of a catalog that has nothing but bio-germicide spray wipes and micro-dusters between the pages of their catalog. But sometimes these products are very difficult to find. They have a large selection of cleaning swabs, for example, which are appropriate for cleaning the heads of a tape drive. There are critical measurements here, and a variety may be what is needed.

**Anthropomorphic Systems, 376 East St. Charles Road, Lombard, IL 60148, 1-800-332-5699.**

This interesting 32-page catalog covers supplies not found anywhere else. It is specifically oriented to software developers, people who need to publish manuals on program operation, and so-called "power users." Anthropomorphic sells customized binders of the type used in microcomputer software packages. They also sell odd-sized paper to fit those binders, custom disk sleeves, labels, and other odd items.

Terms are a little harsh, net 15 days and credit approval in 4-6 weeks! Minimum order is $35.00. These folks are small, and its easy to see why these terms are in effect. Still, you may be able to talk them into more liberal terms.

If you need slip-case binders in IBM format, however, there aren't a great many choices.

## BLACK BOX CATALOG

Black Box deserves special mention as a supplier of telecommunications and cabling equipment:

**Black Box, P.O. Box 12800, Pittsburgh, PA 15241. (412) 746-5530. Minimum order is $20.00. Freight is added, Satisfaction guaranteed, 30 day window. Net 30 days on invoices. Call 8-8 Eastern Time.**

Black Box publishes a catalog of over 150 pages three times a year. They have every data switch imaginable, some of which they have invented, plus a wide variety of telecommunications equipment including spoolers, modems, multiplexers, and line drivers. They are also known for the variety of protocol conversion devices, of which a parallel to serial converter is the least complicated. These are all black boxes, of course.

But that's not all. Black Box also has a range of tools and cabling which will meet most any cabling need. Their prices on crimp-pins are good, and descriptions of the equipment are also top notch.

Indeed, reading the Black Box catalog is an education. Interspersed between part numbers are complete descriptions of the RS232 interface and others, the correct way to crimp pins on to wires. There is enough information between these pages to make an intelligent decision on the products, though a background in the terminology would help.

Certainly anyone involved should get on the Black Box mailing list just for the educational value.

## BOILER ROOM SUPPLIERS

Boiler Rooms are nothing new in the world of business. These are "supply houses" who have people call up an unsuspecting employee and attempt to brow-beat them into ordering products. They operate from a bank of telephones somewhere in the country and canvass certain areas from mailing lists they may purchase from a more legitimate supplier.

The idea is to get one "Yes" answer from an employee, whereupon the goods are shipped, along with an invoice. The "Yes" is obtained by offering to ship to the employee, to their home address, an incentive such as a color television or some other outrageous gift.

The merchandise itself is always incredibly over-priced. A kit of cleaning supplies containing a can of air, a few swabs, and some plastic gloves will retail for $300 per kit, minimum of five per order. This is for merchandise which would otherwise retail for less than $30.00 total. But because this is an introductory offer, the minimum is only three. And if you hesitate, the minimum becomes only one. It can be shipped this very day.

This technique has been used for copy machine supplies ("We just got rid of our machines and have this extra paper to sell at reduced prices.") janitorial supplies (a special soap for the public restrooms) and other office supplies.

The boiler room scam can be recognized by several attributes:

1. The calls will be unsolicited "cold" calls.
2. The sales person will talk to anyone who has a remote connection to ordering.
3. There is an offer of a large gift for trying the product; and they will ask for a home address to send the bribe.
4. There is a constantly changing minimum order required, constantly reduced downward.
5. There will be constant references to questions which tend to solicit a "Yes" answer. ("Don't you think that would be swell?")
6. There will be an assumption that you will order and they simply need a final OK.
7. The prices for the product will be very high.

8. The sales people tend to talk very fast, 4800 baud and up.

One of the better techniques to handle this type of sales approach is to ask if the caller might wait just a moment while stock levels are checked. Place the caller on hold, and leave them there. Telling them they are building up bad karma doesn't seem to help.

# 10 FREE DISK OFFER

## OFFER #1:

Here's how it works. The purchase of this book entitles you to a complete working copy of the inventory program detailed herein. But you get to do some of the work.

For the Inventory Program send one 360K formatted MS-DOS disk along with a return mailer, self-addressed, with sufficient postage to get it back to you.

## OFFER #2:

As should be obvious from Chapter Eight, Jake has figured out the intricacies of CD-ROM disk conflicts. If you would like a free copy of what we call "The Infamous Hoffman Hack," include Another disk. This one is loaded with example files, including batch routines which use the Saywhat screen generator used throughout this book. This takes one disk as well, so if you want both offers, include two disks.

**PROBLEMS WITH FREE OFFERS:**

I have been giving away software for a number of years. Unfortunately, I have encountered difficulty in getting people to understand the requirements. In fact, I now have a stack of disks and mailers over a foot high which have no stamps on them. So please forgive me for emphasizing these small points.

1. 360K Formatted MS-DOS disk: Please format your disk. Make sure it is a 360K disk, not a high density (1.2MB) disk, and not a three and a half inch disk. FORMAT it first, please. We won't refuse you if you forget to format a disk, but we will refuse you if you send the wrong kind.
2. Pack your disk in a self-addressed disk mailer. If you don't have a disk mailer, go to the stationery store and buy one. Disks don't travel well without a disk mailer, composed of sturdy cardboard. They also have a zip-glue strip on them. That makes them easy to mail back. Don't use the glue. Leave the strip on. I get to use the glue, not you.

3. Put your address on the disk mailer under addressee. I might mess up your address, so be sure you do it, not me.
4. Put sufficient postage on the disk mailer. For one disk, this ought to be two or three stamps, depending on the mailer's weight.
5. Be sure to include a note telling me what program you are after. I can probably figure it out, but let's just make sure.
6. Please take a moment to answer the small questionnaire presented in the next section. This is optional, not a requirement for the disk.
7. Place the mailer with the disk into a manila envelope and send it to me. Attempting to reuse your disk mailer may be convenient for you, but it isn't for me.
   Michael Schuyler
   9160 Fox Cove Lane
   Bainbridge Island, WA 98110
8. I will mail you the disks. Easy.

# QUESTIONNAIRE

I also would like you to answer this tiny questionnaire to aid me in analyzing the real-world requirements for computer support. Please take a moment to answer these questions on your own sheet of paper. You may answer just by number if you wish. For example, as an answer to question number one, just write: "1: 16" I'll be able to translate.

I will also keep track of your name and address and mail you a summary of results later on.

1. How many terminals or micros do you support?
2. How many printers do you support?
3. How many FTE (Full Time Equivalent) on your entire staff?
4. How many FTE are devoted to terminal/micro support?
5. How many PCs do you have hooked to a Local Area Network (LAN)?
6. What level of hardware support do you provide? This is independent of software support. We want to know how much responsibility you have for fixing hardware problems. Use the following scale:

Must support a LAN for _____ PCs, score 1.25
We fix everything: 1.00
We fix stuff most of the time:     .8
Some of the time:     .5
Never:     .4

Thank you for answering these questions!

# INDEX

Michael Schuyler is Chief of Support Services at Kitsap Regional Library in Bremerton, Washington. He is the author of numerous articles and books on computer technology including *Now What? How to Get Your Computer Up and Keep it Running*.

Jake Hoffman, Microcomputer Consultant for the State of Idaho since the spring of 1989, was previously Library Automation Coordinator for the Idaho State Library. He is the author of many articles, particularly on CD-ROM, as well as originator of the infamous *Hoffman Hack*—a program which details how to handle CD-ROM conflicts.

Dr. Bill Katz is Professor at the School of Library and Information Science, State University of New York at Albany. He is the author of many distinguished works in library science.

*Book design: Gloria Brown*
*Cover design: Gregory Apicella*
*Typography: Roberts/Churcher*